The Resurrection Life

THE RESURRECTION LIFE

A 40 DAY JOURNEY WITH JESUS

Allen Paul Weaver III, M.Div.

All Scripture quotations, unless otherwise indicated, are taken from the Holy Bible, New International Version®, NIV®. Copyright ©1973, 1978, 1984, 2011 by Biblica, Inc. ™ Used by permission of Zondervan. All rights reserved worldwide. www.zondervan.com The "NIV" and "New International Version" are trademarks registered in the United States Patent and Trademark Office by Biblical, Inc.™

Scripture quotations marked (AMP) are taken fro the Amplified Bible, Copyright © 1954, 1958, 1962, 1964, 1965, 1987 by The Lockman Foundation. Used by permission.

Emphasis added by author in Scripture references indicated by italics, all caps or underline.

ISBN: 978-0-9961045-9-3 Paperback

Published by: Radiant City Studios, LLC

Cover layout and design created by Allen Paul Weaver III
Books may be ordered by contacting: Allen Paul Weaver III at: www.APW3.com

Printed in the United States of America

DEDICATION

This book is written to the glory of Jesus Christ:
the Son of Man of Daniel 7.
LORD, may this devotional help prepare Your
people for Your coming Kingdom.
Amen.

TABLE OF CONTENTS

Prologue
Introduction

PROLOGUE

This book has been a long time coming. For years, I wanted to write a devotional that focused on The Red Letters—the words of Jesus. But the time never seemed to come. Then the Lord blessed me to publish my last book, **Resurrection: The BIG Picture of God's Purpose and Your Destiny.** It released March 2019, just in time for Easter—Resurrection Sunday. Questions arose about what my next book would be... it seemed the time was right to do this devotional as a natural follow up.

Resurrection had helped to provide a focus as I became fascinated with the 40 days Jesus spent with His disciples **after** He rose from the dead on the third day. So, I began to compile various quotes of Jesus and started to write. My plan was to release this book by Easter 2020. Then something strange happened... In the Fall of 2019, the manuscript was about 50% done, but then I suddenly lost interest in finishing the book. I didn't understand why. And then by early 2020, the Covid-19 Coronavirus Pandemic struck the planet!

In the midst of this world-changing chaos, I was focused on trying to co-pastor a church (in addition to taking care of my wife and son). A week before Easter, I had a sudden desire to do something with this manuscript, but didn't know what avenue to take. Then a few days before Easter, my father (who is the senior pastor of the church) called me and said, "I need you to write a 50 day email devotional that can be sent to the congregation, leading from Resurrection Sunday to Pentecost." I told him I had a 40 day devotional I could use and asked if he could write the additional 10 days. He agreed.

So, for 40 days, I adapted most of what was already in my manuscript for these new times we are living in. Along the way, there were several days where the LORD directed me to passages I had not taken notice of before! And even with a manuscript to draw from, this journey was incredibly taxing and amazing at the same time! To be clear, I have never had to write consecutively for 40 days—let alone write something that needed to minister to the lives of others in a trying time. But each day I waited on Jesus... and each day He provided!

When the 40 days of emails were done, several readers suggested I compile them into a book. Look at God... His plans for us often come with a unique path to fulfillment. A path we would not have thought of on our own. He is truly worthy of all the praise, glory and honor!

May the words within these pages help you draw closer to Christ. May you experience His Resurrection Life! The day of His appearing is fast approaching.

-Rev. Allen Paul Weaver III

■■

INTRODUCTION

Resurrection Sunday is the biggest day on the Christian calendar! 40 days of Lent leads believers to The Day we celebrate Christ's victory over death. Jesus' victory has paved the way for *our* victory as well. Yet, for many of us, **THE DAY AFTER** Easter means our lives go back to "business as usual." But, as we deal with the Coronavirus pandemic, "business as usual" is not... *usual*. Even so, these uncertain times actually afford us the opportunity to draw closer to Christ.

So, let's take these next 40 days to dive deeper into the words of Jesus. While doing so, I pray you are encouraged and strengthened in the Lord. After all, Romans 8 tells us that, *"all things work together for the good of those who love the Lord, to those who are the called according to His purpose."* Last time I checked, *"all things"* means **all things**. **The good—The bad—And the ugly.** God is the only one who can take everything in our lives and make it all beautiful for his glory.

Here's the format for each devotional: *day, title, date originally written, opening letter, scripture, commentary, prayer & action. At the end of the book, several 'resurrection thoughts' pages are included for you to write notes.*

Since the very first devotional that was originally emailed fits well with this introduction, it is included in this section to help set the stage for what is to come:

THE MONDAY AFTER...

April 13, 2020

"After his suffering, he presented himself to them and gave many convincing proofs that he was alive. He appeared to them over a period of forty days and spoke about the kingdom of God." - Acts 1:3 New International Version (NIV)

Happy *Monday After* Resurrection Day! You know, Jesus didn't just give His great commission and ascend back to heaven on the day of His resurrection. He didn't leave His disciples to go back to "business as usual." Acts 1:3 reveals that Jesus spent 40 days with His disciples AFTER His resurrection BEFORE returning to heaven to sit at the right hand of God the Father. He taught and impressed upon His disciples the reality of God's Kingdom and their place in it. He prepared them for their life-long mission.

Jesus took this time to explain how all Scripture centers around and points to Him as the Son of God, the Son of Man and the Savior, Lord and King of the World. Imagine the conversations that were had between Jesus and His disciples! Imagine the miracles He performed!

The number 40 is significant in the Bible. For our purposes I will focus on two instances: Jesus spent 40 days preparing at the beginning of His earthly ministry; and He spent 40 days *preparing His disciples* at the conclusion of His earthly ministry. I would imagine spending 40 days of intense focus on ANY endeavor would yield some kind of growth, breakthrough and potentially life-changing experience.

Have you ever spent 40 consecutive days with the resurrected Jesus and His teachings? Let's continue to learn more about why Jesus' crucifixion and resurrection are critical to our eternal destiny and our purpose here on earth.

ACTION: Commit to spending the next 40 days with the LORD through reading this devotional and meditating on its truths.

PRAYER: Heavenly Father, over the next 40 days, please help me draw closer to You through Your Son, Jesus. Open my eyes, heart and mind to receive Your truth. For I know this is the desire of Your heart. In Jesus' Name I pray, Amen.

DAY 1

HAVING EYES TO SEE

April 14, 2020

As we stay in our homes watching the news about the Covid-19 Coronavirus, I am reminded of a quote by Helen Keller. ***"The only thing worse than being blind is having sight but no vision."*** Helen Keller was blind and deaf, yet she was an author, political activist, a well traveled lecturer. She did not allow her lack of sight to restrict her vision. Nor did she allow her disabled hearing to keep her from listening.

Right now, our physical sight and hearing may be clouded with images of loss and fear. But the Bible teaches that the people of God are not limited to physical sight and hearing. Jesus said that He did what He saw his Father do. He also encouraged those who had ears to hear to listen for the movement of the Holy Spirit. Covid-19 does not have the last word. God does. Let us look and listen through the filter God provides by reading, meditating and praying through the Scriptures. Then, we will see and hear in a way that brings God glory.

Jesus is worthy of all praise and worship!

25 He said to them, "How foolish you are, and how slow to believe all that the prophets have spoken! 26 Did not the Messiah have to suffer these things and then enter his glory?" 27 And beginning with Moses and all the Prophets, he explained to them what was said in all the Scriptures concerning himself. — Luke 24: 25-27 (NIV)

The disciples did not understand what was happening. The man they believed to be the Messiah was dead. All of their expectations about Jesus — *who they thought He was and what they thought He came to do* — were dashed to pieces. They were broken and disillusioned by His crucifixion, which seemed to be a complete failure. And when the two disciples unknowingly encountered Jesus on the road to Emmaus, they shared their dismay and revealed their lack of faith and understanding. They did not have eyes to see...

But, what did Jesus do? He pointed out their area of lack and then began to *build* and *strengthen* them by taking them through the Scriptures. Jesus taught them from the Word! Do not think because Jesus calls out your areas of weakness, that He is displeased with you to the point of casting you away. *He tells you the truth because He loves you and wants you to grow in Him!* The Holy Spirit will cause you to grow in faith as you learn and understand the Scriptures.

Jesus makes it clear that the entire Old Testament was about Him. We already know the entire New Testament is about Him as well. As we seek to grow closer to Christ, let us make time to study God's Word — *having eyes to see the clues left by Christ on every page and in every story.* Then, with excitement and anticipation, we will experience the Holy Spirit growing our faith in Christ so we can be equipped for whatever lies ahead.

PRAYER: Heavenly Father, please help me to see the Grand Story in the Bible about Your Son. In Jesus' Name. Amen.

ACTION: Study what Moses & the prophets say about Jesus.

DAY 2

KNOWING THE FATHER THROUGH THE SON
April 15, 2020

We often discover in crisis how much we *really* know. It is also when we find out the identity of our *real* friends. Before crisis—we know things and people on one level. That level is often shallow. But during and after a crisis—our knowledge deepens.

In John 16:33, Jesus tells us that we will have many struggles in this life. But we can have joy, hope and peace because He has overcome the world. His words are an *invitation* to *know* Him at a deeper level... that level where negative circumstances do not diminish our faith.

As you will see in today's devotional, there is always more to learn about God because He is inexhaustible! It is when things get difficult and we are forced to our knees, that we find out just how much our Heavenly Father loves us, is with us and provides for us. May we all receive Christ's invitation to know Him deeper during this time.

<u>Jesus is worthy of the praise and the glory!</u>

"Now this is eternal life: that they know you, the only true God, and Jesus Christ, whom you have sent." - John 17:3 (NIV)

When I stop to seriously consider Jesus' words... I realize there is a level of relationship God makes available to believers that we have rarely—if ever—experienced. **Jesus reveals to**

us a marvelous truth about eternal life: *it is the result of knowing God the Father and God the Son.* He spoke about this reality during His earthly ministry:

"Jesus answered, 'I am the way and the truth and the life. No one comes to the Father except through Me.'" - John 14:6

"I have made you known to them, and will continue to make you known in order that the love you have for Me may be in them and that I Myself may be in them." -John 17:26

"Jesus replied, 'Anyone who loves Me will obey My teaching. My Father will love them, and we will come to them and make our home with them.'" - John 14:23

"I and the Father are one." - John 10:30

Jesus makes it clear that eternal life is found in a *direct relationship* with Himself. He is the source of all life. He is in *direct relationship* with His Heavenly Father. He *invites us* to be *a part of that relationship* as well—through His Word and through prayer.

"...That all of them may be one, Father, just as you are in Me and I am in you. May they also be in us so that the world may believe that you have sent Me." - John 17:21

We often think about the "things" God has in store for us— money, house, car, *etc—but do we think about the depth of relationship God desires to have with us?* There is a loving oneness between the Father and the Son that Jesus says we *can* experience: <u>a oneness between us and God and one another.</u> There are no schisms between the Father, the Son and the Holy Spirit. As we grow closer to Christ *together*, the schisms we experience between one another will diminish.

4

This kind of *loving oneness isn't* just for us alone, but so the world may know that the Father has sent His Son as Lord and Savior of humanity.

When you have a relationship *with* God <u>you have God's eternal life as well.</u> His life in you will lead you to your purpose. His life in you will make you stand out in dark times. His life in you will sustain you—in wondrous ways—now and for all eternity. Don't just settle for knowing *about* God. Through Christ, an ever deepening relationship with the Father is possible! It is reserved, as a spiritual birthright, for each of us who believe.

PRAYER: Heavenly Father, teach us how to know You through Your Son, Jesus. Amen.

ACTION: Share what you are learning about Christ with those you know.

DAY 3

BELIEVE THE GOOD NEWS

April 16, 2020

Each day we await some kind of news—often hoping for a big break to pursue our dreams. We also hope in life that the scales of good news will outweigh the scales of bad news. Just over a month ago, the news we were waiting for had nothing to do with the Covid-19 Coronavirus. Now, practically all the news we see and hear is related to the pandemic the world is currently facing.

Everything has changed. Our focus has shifted. But Hebrews 13:8 reminds us that there is Someone who never changes: *"Jesus Christ is the same yesterday and today and forever."* With everything that is going on in our world and in our lives, it's good to be reminded about the ultimate Good News!

Jesus is worthy of all of our praise and worship!

"After John was put in prison, Jesus went into Galilee, proclaiming the good news of God. "The time has come," he said. "The kingdom of God has come near. Repent and believe the good news." -Mark 1:14-15

Jesus goes out and preaches *after* hearing that John the Baptist was put in prison. He doesn't speak to the prison guard on John's behalf. He doesn't break him out. He doesn't even send an angel to his rescue. John is disillusioned by the unexpected turn of events. At the height of his ministry, he

6

boldly declared who Jesus was: "The Lamb of God who takes away the sin of the world." Now, at his lowest point, he sends his followers to ask Jesus, "are you the one or should we look for another?"

Jesus tells John to remain focused on the reality of what he has seen and heard: *the Good News*. John didn't realize prison and death-by-beheading would fulfill God's purpose for his life. Crisis tested his beliefs and convictions. But once he received Jesus' response and regained his focus on the mission, John faithfully endured until the end of his earthly journey—and no doubt received his heavenly reward!

The *Good News* is **infinitely greater** than all other news! It reaches deeper than any earthly sadness. It soars higher than any earthly joy! You can trace it back to Genesis 3:15 where God judges the serpent (*Satan)* and proclaims the future day when a Savior will destroy evil and free humanity! Revelation 14:6 declares that the *Good News* is eternal! God's plan of salvation stretches back before the universe began and extends into God's great unknown. How? Because Christ is eternal and the *Good News* is all about Him.

Have you ever wondered why, after Jesus rose from the dead, that His body is completely healed, but the scars from the cross remain?

We will forever look upon the One who saved us and see the scars. We will forever remember the price God paid to redeem us! And we will be forever grateful. JESUS is *The Good News!*

"That God was reconciling the world to Himself in Christ, not counting people's sins against them. And He has committed to us the message of reconciliation." -2 Corinthians 5:19

This was Christ's central message: _That God had entered into our human story in such a unique way to finally carry out what He had promised so long ago._ I say "finally" because we humans often have problems with time. Yet God, who is not limited by time and space, has no such issues. When we have to wait a long time on God, _we can become disillusioned. Then we find other things... lesser things... to try and fill our lives with some sense of alternative meaning._ But these things are poor substitutes for what we truly need.

God will allow failures in our life. Some will be because we did not do what is right. Others will be because we did something right. However, Christ lets us know repeatedly, that whatever we lose in this life in order to follow God's plan for us, we will regain with interest in the resurrection!

PRAYER: Heavenly Father, please help me to trust You when things don't go how I expect. When plans fall apart, may You hold me together so that my faith in Jesus does not fail. Amen

ACTION: Search the Scriptures to find those individuals who faced unexpected turn of events. Find out how they retained or regained their faith in God.

DAY 4

TEACH US TO PRAY

April 17, 2020

Prayer is both a great privilege and a great responsibility. In 26 years of ministry many have asked me to pray for them. Early on I would ask what they desired and prayed accordingly. However, over time God has taught me that sometimes our desires are not in line with His plans. How has He taught me this truth? There have been times when I have prayed for someone's physical healing and they have miraculously gotten better. There have been *other* times however, when I have prayed for someone's physical recovery… and they have died. These outcomes have been rough, causing me to wrestle with God for understanding.

This wrestling has caused me to acknowledge that God has His own infinite plan which He is carrying out in every life across the world. And His plan stretches from time into eternity. And although I may not always understand what He is doing, God's track record has proven that He is trustworthy. And so, I pray with the assurance that He will intervene *some way, some how*, when I call on Him. Whether that means He changes the situation or helps me get through it.

As you live from day-to-day, know that God will do the same for you. He is working out all things in your life for His glory and your good. May this devotional help increase both your understanding of prayer and your desire to pray.

Jesus is worthy of all praise, glory and honor!

9 "In this manner, therefore, pray: Our Father in heaven, hallowed be Your name, 10 Your kingdom come. Your will be done on earth as it is in heaven. 11 Give us this day our daily bread. 12 And forgive us our debts, as we forgive our debtors. 13 And do not lead us into temptation, but deliver us from the evil one. For Yours is the kingdom and the power and the glory forever. Amen." - Matthew 6:9-13 (NKJV)

Either we pray or we do not. We often spend more time complaining about our circumstances than we do praying to God about them. And if we do pray, we may have no idea what it means to truly "pray according to God's will." We pray according to *our own will* and hope God changes His mind in order to fulfill our desires.

But what about God's Will? Is it hard to know it? What about what He desires? 1 John 5:14 states: *"This is the confidence we have in approaching God: that if we ask anything according to His will, He hears us."* Clearly, God wants us to pray in a way that agrees with His Will and brings Him glory, honor and even pleasure. Through His word and example, Jesus provides the framework for us to learn how to do this. For this truth to work in our lives, we must first *see ourselves in* His disciples.

In Luke 11, where this prayer is also recorded, we find the disciples had approached Jesus. They had this nagging feeling after watching Jesus pray. Even though they were with Jesus, something was still missing: they were operating at a spiritual deficit. They also saw John's disciples praying and couldn't take it anymore. Instead of trying to cover up their lack, one of them makes a desperate request on behalf of the group: "Lord, teach us to pray as John taught his disciples to pray."

Surely, they prayed on occasion: perhaps over their food or when encountering a crisis. But this was different. They were fighting against their own sense of self-will and self-sufficiency. They wanted to be enraptured in something larger than themselves; what had to this point been foreign to them. And so, Jesus teaches them to pray.

For everyone who says "I don't know what to pray," Jesus gives us the words and the order. Both are important. Although it's listed as the "Lord's Prayer," it is really the *"Prayer the Lord provides for His disciples to follow."* <u>Each line of Matthew 6:9-13 can be broken down:</u>

*Acknowledge God's Name, His holiness and His sovereign position.

*Seek and surrender to God's Kingdom intervention and Will.

*Ask God to provide your daily provisions.

*Ask God to forgive you for your sins and to give you the ability to forgive others.

*Ask God to lead you away from things (internal/external) that will pull you from Him.

*Ask God to deliver you from physical and spiritual attacks of evil.

*Acknowledge that God owns all creation and is working all things out for His glory.

Notice that God is the primary focus of the prayer. The prayer begins with God, continues with God and ends with God. He is both the Director and the Main Character and we are the supporting roles. And as we pray according to the example Christ provides, we will find God drawing us near—every closer—as our will surrenders to His. And whenever we pray according to God's will, the answer will always be yes!

Finally, we cannot just run through this prayer and "check off" that we hit all the categories. Prayer *takes* time. So, *make* time. We make time for what is important to us. Prayer, *the way Jesus intends it to be*, is of the utmost importance to the life of the Christian! God is waiting to meet with you in intimate communion through prayer.

PRAYER: Heavenly Father, thank you for providing a strong example in Your word on how to pray! Help me to know that when I pray according to Your will You hear me and will respond. In Jesus' Name. Amen.

ACTION: For every action you complain about… pray about.

DAY 5

LET CHRIST BREATHE ON YOU

April 18, 2020

We don't realize how necessary breathing is until we can't do it. Whether it's an asthma attack, choking or drowning—when we can't breathe, nothing else matters except our next breath. Dreams and aspirations are hardly in focus. Even grudges fall away. In these moments we realize just how fragile we are and how precious life is.

When I was in college, a student named Henry had an asthma attack. I considered him an enemy, but this experience broke my resentment. Another student and I tried to calm him down before he passed out. Seconds seemed like hours waiting for the ambulance to arrive. He almost died in front of us. Tears streamed down my face as I asked God for forgiveness. When Henry came back from the hospital, I asked him to forgive me, too. We became friends. Months later the Lord saved him. A few weeks after that, he was tragically killed. I look forward to seeing Henry again at the Resurrection.

Today's devotional is about Jesus breathing on us. If needing oxygen in our lungs is important, then needing the breath of God's Spirit in our souls is paramount.

Jesus is worthy of all praise, worship and honor!

"Again Jesus said, "Peace be with you! As the Father has sent Me, I am sending you." And with that He breathed on them and said, 'Receive the Holy Spirit.'" -John 20:21-22 (NIV)

It was the evening of Christ's resurrection. The disciples were in a locked room fearing for their lives. That morning Mary Magdalene told them she saw Jesus—alive! According to Luke 24, two of the disciples were leaving town when Jesus encountered them on the road. He opened up their understanding of the Scriptures and showed how the Messiah had to die and then rise to life on the 3rd day. They rushed back to Jerusalem—to the group—declaring Jesus was alive! Still, not everyone believed.

That evening, in a locked room, Jesus appeared to the group. They thought He was a ghost! But He let them touch His body so they could see He was flesh and blood. They were speechless as Jesus spoke to them: *"Peace be with you! As the Father has sent Me, I am sending you."* He breathed on them and said, *"Receive the Holy Spirit."* Jesus' *sending* has not changed. If we belong to Him, then He sends us!

It is amazing to consider that Jesus sends us in the *same manner* that His Father sent Him. He was sent into this fallen world to rescue humanity. He sends us into the world as His "ambassadors of reconciliation" to tell others about His redeeming power. Jesus was sent to re-establish an eternal relationship between God and people. He sends us to demonstrate *that relationship,* so others would desire to know Him. Jesus' mission was literally LOVE in action. If we belong to Him, then His LOVE should course through our veins with increasing intensity over time.

It is by the Holy Spirit that Christ *continues His mission through us*. This Christian life is impossible without His indwelling. Jesus wants to breathe on you as He did with His first disciples. His breathing is reminiscent of Genesis 2:7. There, God breathed His Spirit into the lifeless body of the first human. And that man, Adam, became a living being! Life without God's Spirit in us is really no life at all. Without God's Spirit we are incapable of knowing and worshiping Him in spirit and in truth. We are also unable to accomplish the full purpose for which we were created.

In Luke 11:13, Jesus tells us that His Father desires to give us His Holy Spirit. He wants to restore His intimate relationship! There is a baptism of the Spirit that is available to *every* believer. This is where God makes His Presence directly accessible to each of us for the purpose of bringing eternal glory to His Kingdom! Yes, the glory you bring to Christ today will last forever! So, continue to put yourself in a position, posture and environment to receive. Surrender your plans to Him, seek His face and learn how to rely on the power and Presence of Christ each day. Imagine what's possible when we receive what our Heavenly Father so desires to give! Let Christ breathe on you...

PRAYER: Heavenly Father, please breathe on me with Your Holy Spirit so I may live in the way You desire. In Jesus' Name. Amen.

ACTION: When you read the Scriptures and encounter a passage you don't understand, ask Jesus to open your understanding by the Holy Spirit. Then spend time studying that passage with the Holy Spirit as your Teacher.

DAY 6

WAIT FOR THE GIFT

April 19, 2020

The weeks leading up to our son's 6th birthday were very difficult. He knew we were taking him to iFly, a vertical wind tunnel facility. He inherited my love of flight and had watched videos of myself and others flying on a cushion of air. With each passing day, our son felt like he was going to burst at the seams! His birthday couldn't come fast enough. A few days before his Big Day, he had enough! He no longer wanted to wait. Now, excited anticipation had turned into a sort of negative anxiety.

To help calm him down, I took him to iFly a couple of days before his birthday so he could see first hand what things would be like. As God would have it, the place was almost empty and the flight instructor gave my son a personal performance. My son was amazed beyond his wildest dreams. That experience helped him reach his birthday unscathed by impatience. And what an experience we had on his Big Day.

While you are waiting on God during this time of Covid-19, don't allow impatience to overwhelm you. You may have been bold at the beginning of this ordeal, but find your faith waning due to the news of increased deaths and unemployment. Trust God's process and His track record in your life! Use this time to get ready for what God has reserved for you each day. All things work together for God's glory and for the good of those who love Him.

Jesus is worthy of all praise, worship and honor!

"On one occasion, while he was eating with them, he gave them this command: 'Do not leave Jerusalem, but wait for the gift my Father promised, which you have heard me speak about... But you will receive power when the Holy Spirit comes on you; and you will be my witnesses in Jerusalem, and in all Judea and Samaria, and to the ends of the earth." -Acts 1:4,8 (NIV)

Imagine spending 40 days with Jesus—after His resurrection. Imagine the times of teaching, the questions and answers, the miracles and yes... the many meals and fellowship! As the 40 days drew to a close, Jesus told his disciples to wait for the outpouring of the Holy Spirit. They needed to have the supernatural power and guidance necessary to continue His work on earth. ***Jesus' command to wait for power has not changed.*** It applies to every follower of Christ.

God gives the plan. He also gives the power and provision to carry out the plan. We must take time to wait on the power of the Holy Spirit. Depending on the situation, that wait time could be long or short. Realize, if we could do the work on our own, then Jesus wouldn't have told us to wait for His Spirit. Do not let the urgency of the situation cause you to run ahead of God. Do not allow the suggestions of others cause you to get ahead of God. Learn how to wait until God gives you the green light to move.

"Those who wait on the LORD will renew their strength. They shall mount up with wings like an eagle. They shall run and not grow weary. They shall walk and not faint." (Isaiah 40:31)

Waiting doesn't mean you and I are just sitting on the couch binge-watching our favorite tv shows. When the disciples waited, they spent much time in prayer, the Scriptures and rehearsing the plans Jesus gave them. In other words, *a time of waiting is a time of development.* It's a time to develop perspective, patience, strategy and an inner conviction to get the job done. It is a time to specifically seek God for His Presence, guidance and power. It is *never* about doing nothing. It is *always* about getting in the right position and posture to receive what God desires to give.

If the disciples had chosen not to wait, they would have not received God's power. If they had decided to wait in a place *other than* where Jesus told them, they would not have received God's power. If they had started to wait, but quit before the Holy Spirit was given, they would not have received God's power.

The key is to be obedient to Jesus' command. Sometimes the command is location and time specific! **Don't think you can receive from God *at any time* if He has declared a timeframe and place where He wants to meet you.** For example, a time of prayer may be called at your church. Do not neglect the time nor the location. A blessing is waiting for you there. In our case now, because of Covid-19, God has called us to seek His face from our homes. Don't waste this unprecedented opportunity by spending more time doing other things. Press your way to be obedient to the command of Jesus. Continue to draw near to Him today.

PRAYER: Heavenly Father, please provide Your plan, power & provision for my life so I may bring You glory. In Jesus' Name. Amen.

ACTION: Carve out time in your week to draw near to God.

DAY 7

THEN YOU WILL FIND SOME

April 20, 2020

Jesus says in John 15:7-9, "If you remain in Me and My words remain in you, ask whatever you wish, and it will be done for you. 8 This is to My Father's glory, that you bear much fruit, proving yourselves to be My disciples. 9 As the Father has loved Me, so have I loved you. Remain in My love..."

Our Heavenly Father desires for us to bring Him glory. The greatest glory is when we trust Him by trusting His Son. Whatever situation you face, look for Jesus to speak to you. And then do what He tells you to do. The primary way God speaks is through His Word, the Bible. He will never tell you to do something that contradicts what is already written. This is why it is so important to remain in Christ by allowing the Scriptures to remain in you.

Jesus is worthy of all praise, glory and honor!

"He said, "Throw your net on the right side of the boat and you will find some." When they did, they were unable to haul the net in because of the large number of fish." - John 21:6 (NIV)

We believe God for the "BIG" things: creating the universe. Sustaining all life. Salvation which lasts forever. But we often act like we know better than God when He tells us to do something that is counter-intuitive to our way of thinking. We rely more on our limited experience than on God's infinite

19

knowledge about ALL experiences. We live our day-to-day lives based on "facts" rather than based on God's truth.

The "facts" were that the disciples had spent all night fishing. The "facts" were that even with their best efforts they caught nothing. The "facts" were that many of them were trained fishermen. Then Jesus comes along the shore and calls out to them about the "facts." "Friends, haven't you any fish?" At first they don't realize it is Him. They reply with the "facts." "No." Then He tells them to do what *doesn't make sense*. "Throw your net on the right side of the boat and you will find some."

Was it that simple? All they needed to do was switch sides? Did the fish not like the left side of the boat and so they determined to only respond to the right side? Not at all. It wasn't that the fish favored one side or the other. It was that the fish responded to the command of their Creator. Jesus could have told the disciples to hold the net open IN the boat and the fish would have jumped in!

The question is, **will we listen to Jesus' command, especially when it doesn't make sense?** Will we follow through with His desires or try to accomplish things on our own? It isn't that Jesus ignores the facts—they matter. But Jesus is greater than mere human facts. If He tells us to act, then what matters most is being obedient to His command. This account in the Scriptures shows that Jesus desires for us to "do life" with Him instead of always "flying solo." He loves us and desires to meet our needs. But He doesn't do it so we can run away and forget about Him. He helps us so we can see Him for who He truly is: *our Lord and Savior.*

So, the disciples obey the command and cast their net on the right side of the boat. Then the miracle happened! There were actually *two* miracles—one greater than the other. The first was that the fish filled the net. The greater miracle was that they recognized it was Jesus standing on the sea shore. It makes me wonder if I always recognize Christ when He stands on the sea shore of my life and provides for me? What about you?

This was the second time Jesus had done this miracle for His disciples. Each time it was to draw their attention, their allegiance, their adoration and their love to Him. And it is perfectly natural for the Creator and Sustainer of the universe to desire this from His creation. After all, we were created in God's image for the purpose of being in an intimate relationship with God the Father, the Son and the Holy Spirit.

Are you trusting Jesus for the "BIG" things—like your salvation —but have problems trusting Him to help you meet your day-to-day responsibilities? He is fully capable of doing both!

Do these three things to grow your ability to trust God:

ONE: Pray and ask Jesus to help grow your ability to trust Him in every situation. (Matthew 7:7-8 / Luke 17:5-6)

TWO: Make time to read the Bible on a consistent basis, so Jesus can build faith in you through the Holy Spirit. (John 6:63 / Romans 10:17 / Hebrews 12:2)

THREE: Seek counsel from God's Word for every situation and put the Word into practice. (Proverbs 3:5-6 / James 1:22-25)

PRAYER: Heavenly Father, please help me to obey Your commands—especially when they don't make sense to my way of thinking. In Jesus' Name. Amen.

ACTION: When dealing with a situation, list the "facts" and seek God's commands about it.

DAY 8

EVEN IN DEATH WE BRING GOD GLORY

April 21, 2020

Sometimes I don't have words to help bring comfort to those who are grieving. But I am grateful God's Word is always appropriate. Read 1 Thessalonians 4:13-18:

"13 Brothers and sisters, we do not want you to be uninformed about those who sleep in death, so that you do not grieve like the rest of mankind, who have no hope. 14 For we believe that Jesus died and rose again, and so we believe that God will bring with Jesus those who have fallen asleep in him. 15 According to the Lord's word, we tell you that we who are still alive, who are left until the coming of the Lord, will certainly not precede those who have fallen asleep. 16 For the Lord himself will come down from heaven, with a loud command, with the voice of the archangel and with the trumpet call of God, and the dead in Christ will rise first. 17 After that, we who are still alive and are left will be caught up together with them in the clouds to meet the Lord in the air. And so we will be with the Lord forever. 18 Therefore encourage one another with these words."

This is our heritage and our hope as saints of God! In Christ, death is just like falling asleep. It doesn't hurt to fall asleep. And when we get a good night's sleep, we rise in the morning refreshed, ready to burst forth on the day. And oh, what a bursting forth it will be when Christ resurrects us all with new bodies at the moment of His coming!

Jesus is worthy of all the praise, glory and honor!

"Very truly I tell you, when you were younger you dressed yourself and went where you wanted; but when you are old you will stretch out your hands, and someone else will dress you and lead you where you do not want to go." Jesus said this to indicate the kind of death by which Peter would glorify God. Then he said to him, "Follow me!" - John 21:18-19 (NIV)

Before the crucifixion, Peter had denied three times that he knew Jesus. Even though he previously declared he would die for Jesus, when the possibility arose, he was overcome with fear and refused to even be associated with Him. Now, after Jesus' resurrection He asked Peter three times (*John 21:15-17*), "Do you love Me?" This was how Jesus restored Peter back into full fellowship. Then, as they walked the sea shore, Jesus brought up a touchy subject: the circumstances surrounding how Peter would die.

We all have to die—unless Jesus comes back first. Ever since Adam and Eve ate the forbidden fruit in the Garden of Eden, death has been inevitable. But for those of us who serve God, even our deaths can bring Him glory. Yes, you read correctly: *even our deaths...* We often want to bring God glory with our life. We pray for opportunities to do GREAT THINGS for Him. We want to do BIG THINGS that point people to Christ. We want to be blessed so we can tell others it was Jesus who provided... the new car, new house, new job, new child, new church building, new healing, new... new... new...

But have you ever stopped to seriously consider how God will use your death to bring Him glory? I know, this seems a bit morbid. No one really wants to sit and think about how they are going to die. We often spend time fearing death and trying to figure out how to stop it from coming. We even list the ways

23

in which *we don't want to die.* Personally, I'd rather lie down in my bed and peacefully close my eyes and die in my sleep—only to open my eyes in eternity looking into the face of Jesus. I think we all would like to transition from earth to heaven in this fashion.

Sadly, during this time of Covid-19 many have had to deal with the death of a friend or loved one PLUS an additional complication:**we can't say goodbye.** Due to the infectious nature of the virus, men, women and children have died in isolation. They have been in hospital rooms, in senior centers and in their homes. Family members haven't been allowed to be present! We couldn't talk to them, hug them, kiss them, hold them. This has made an already terrible situation even worse! Right now, as you read these words, you may have gone through this very scenario or know of someone who has! But let me encourage you from the Scriptures. **The Bible is clear that those who belong to God DO NOT die alone!**

"Precious in the sight of the LORD is the death of his faithful servants." - Psalm 116:15

"Now it happened that the poor man died and his spirit was carried away by the angels to Abraham's bosom (paradise)..." - Luke 16:22a

"And if I go and prepare a place for you, I will come back and take you to be with me that you also may be where I am." - John 14:3

These Scriptures are true! And I have heard stories which attest to them—where believers—just before the moment of their death—have either seen angels or Jesus Himself coming to receive them to their eternal home! Understand that God loves each of us INFINITELY MORE than we love each other.

And He is not only with those we can't be with... He is also with us who mourn their passing and He promises to comfort us with His Holy Spirit.

According to Psalm 139:16 and Job 14:5, God has determined the day of our birth, the number of days we will live on this earth, *and* the day of our death. And we can rest in knowing that nothing happens to us that takes God by surprise. This allows us to contemplate how we can bring God glory in life and in death.

After Jesus told Peter how he would die, He then told him, "Follow Me!" And that's the question we are left with each day: ***Will we follow Jesus wherever He leads us, no matter what the final outcome of our earthly life will be?***

PRAYER: Heavenly Father, I don't know how many days I have left on earth. But You do. I ask that You give me Your peace for each day. May You get the glory out of my life, as well as out of my death. For I believe that death does not have the last word because I belong to You. In Jesus' Name. Amen.

ACTION: Make a list of the ways you think you may die and the ways you don't want to die. Confront them in prayer by giving them over to Christ. Ask Him to make you ready for the day of your departure... whenever it may be. And ask Him to give you the courage to live fully as He desires.

DAY 9

CONTEMPLATING THE LORD'S GLORY

April 22, 2020

How are you spending your time? It's so easy to spend the majority of our time watching nonstop news coverage of the latest Coronavirus developments. But don't do it! What we spend the majority of our time focusing on is what will have the greatest sway over our mind, will and emotions.

I was glued to the television during the first week of sheltering-in-place. For the first several days I watched the morning news, the 12 noon news, the 4pm news, the 5pm news, the 6pm news, World News Tonight at 6:30pm, the 10pm news and then the 11 o'clock news! By that Thursday, I was having a flareup of Shingles symptoms and didn't know why? Then I remembered that stress is a trigger.

The Lord convicted me. I was spending more time focusing on the Pandemic than I was on Him. The result? Stress was building up. Instead of watching the news that night, I put headphones on, listened to the Scriptures on my Dwell Bible app and prayed. I fell asleep to the Word. When I woke up Friday morning, my mind was at peace and the flareup was gone (and hasn't come back)! What we focus on matters. Today's devotional will help you see that. Let's focus on God through His Word.

Christ is worthy of all praise, glory and honor!

"And we all, who with unveiled faces contemplate the Lord's glory, are being transformed into his image with ever-increasing glory, which comes from the Lord, who is the Spirit." -2 Corinthians 3:18 (NIV)

This **Scripture is clear...** *we are to contemplate the glory of the Lord in order to grow in being conformed to His image.* In other words, we are transformed by what we set our eyes, ears and minds on. But how much time do we spend contemplating the things of the world in comparison to the things of Christ?

When my son was a baby, he loved carrot baby food. He loved it so much that he would eat it almost exclusively. Then one day my wife and I noticed his nose had a very noticeable orange tint. So did other parts of his body, like his fingernails. When my wife took him to the pediatrician for a checkup, he looked at our son's nose and said, "Lay off the carrots. He's eating too much."

Our son was becoming a carrot! "You are what you eat." At least figuratively, but in some ways it is literal too. What we eat... or rather what we contemplate has an affect on us. It changes who we are over time. So, if Scripture tells us that as we contemplate the Lord's glory we are in fact being transformed—by the mere act of focusing and reflecting—then this truth also applies to **anything** we contemplate: movies, tv shows, music, violence, lust, pride, etc. What we put before our eyes and train our mind on affects how we think, how we act, our development and who we ultimately become.

The word "contemplate" is defined as: *to look thoughtfully for a long time at; to think about; to think profoundly about something at length.*

What do you spend your time contemplating? It is interesting that when Albert Einstein talked about his uncanny ability to solve extremely complex problems he said, *"It's not that I'm so smart, it's just that I stay with problems longer."* He realized the power of contemplation!

The average Christian can talk for hours about the things of this world (their interests, dreams, aspirations, problems), but can barely speak for minutes at a time about the things of God. This shows us what truly captures our heart. How much time do you spend contemplating the attributes of Jesus Christ as revealed in the Scriptures? What wonders are waiting to be revealed if we would just increase our focus on the One the entire Bible is written about?

PRAYER: Heavenly Father, please increase my appetite and desire for spiritual matters. Help me spend more time contemplating Your truth. In Jesus' Name. Amen.

ACTION: Whatever your level of Bible reading and prayer, increase it by a minimum of 5-10 minutes a day.

DAY 10

THE RESURRECTION LIFE

April 23, 2020

We are often encouraged to have a plan. We are asked, "what's your 1-year-plan?" "Do you have a 3-5 year plan?" "What do you plan to do with your life?" "Where do you plan to be this time next year?" One thing is for sure, last year we did not plan to be here dealing with this Covid-19 Coronavirus!

Here's what James 4:13-15 says: *"**13** Now listen, you who say, 'Today or tomorrow we will go to this or that city, spend a year there, carry on business and make money.' **14** Why, you do not even know what will happen tomorrow. What is your life? You are a mist that appears for a little while and then vanishes. **15** Instead, you ought to say, 'If it is the Lord's will, we will live and do this or that.'"*

There is a commercial on television which says, "the only way to plan for the future is to create it." Yet, Ephesians 2:10 says: *"For we are God's handiwork, created in Christ Jesus to do good works, which God prepared in advance for us to do."* Here we see the difference between the wisdom of the world and the wisdom of God. We can either try to plan and create our own future *or* we can seek the One who created us with a *future* in mind. We can either try to be self-sufficient *or* we can learn how to become *God-sufficient* through the resurrection life He provides for us. My hope and prayer is that you seek the latter.

Jesus is worthy of all the praise, glory and honor!

29

"You should not be surprised at my saying, 'You must be born again.' The wind blows wherever it pleases. You hear its sound, but you cannot tell where it comes from or where it is going. So it is with everyone born of the Spirit." - John 3:7-8 (NIV)

"In their hearts humans plan their course, but the LORD establishes their steps." -Proverbs 16:9 (NIV)

"Paul and his companions traveled throughout the region of Phrygia and Galatia, having been kept by the Holy Spirit from preaching the word in the province of Asia." -Acts 16:6 (NIV)

My former pastor, Rev. Dr. Shellie Sampson Jr, would often say, *"Make your plans, but always leave room for the Holy Spirit to show up."*

Acts 16:6 actually gives us a glimpse of Proverbs 16:9 at work. It would seem that the apostle Paul planned his way—he was going on a missionary journey—but the Holy Spirit **ordered** his steps. The first few locations Paul picked, the Holy Spirit said, *"No."* Why? Because God has a plan for how He wants His message to be spread to the world. Such is the life of a person who is led by the Spirit. At many times it is a slow pace because *as* we plan, we also *have to* wait on God's plan. We have to wait for direction, for power and for provision. But when God says, *"Go,"* then things can move as quick as a rushing wind!

So, what did Paul do after the Lord shut the door on his plans? No doubt *he prayed*. And then, according to Acts 16:9, one night he had a vision of a man from Macedonia asking him to come and help them. Paul awoke from the vision, knowing what the Lord wanted him to do. He immediately got to work walking the path the Holy Spirit had laid out before him!

In John 3, Jesus told Nicodemus that the person who is led by the Spirit is like the wind. You don't know which direction the wind is coming from or going. It is mysterious. So, is everyone who is born of the Spirit. God often **moves** us in unexpected ways... **Unexpected to us**, *but not to Him.*

Salvation is mysterious. The godly life is mysterious. Resurrection is mysterious. We don't exactly know *how* they work, but we can see *the evidence of them working* in all those who truly surrender to the lordship of Jesus Christ. There is always an element of surprise as to how things are going to work out. But things *do* work out because God will see to it that His Word and purposes come to pass. *(Jeremiah 1:12)*

"'For my thoughts are not your thoughts, neither are your ways my ways,' declares the LORD." -Isaiah 55:8 (NIV)

God is **extremely creative** in how He carries out His purposes! Often, His plans for us come to pass in ways we do not expect! So, don't try to overthink things—where you seek to control every aspect of every element and have a contingency plan for each contingency plan. You will only frustrate yourself. Don't try to chisel your life plans in stone. God will always break down the idols we create. **The resurrection life is not chiseled in stone, but is written in the depths of human hearts.** Some of the most meaningful experiences you will have in life will be *accidents* to you, but *deliberately ordained moments* by God.

Only God sees everything, knows everything and has all power over everything. So, don't presume to automatically know what God's plans are. Put your trust in Him. Place your plans in His hands. Follow where He leads and His plans for your life will increase in clarity with the passage of each day.

PRAYER: Heavenly Father, I am grateful that You have a plan and purpose for me. I give You my plans in favor of Your own. Help me to trust that Your plans are better than anything I could come up with on my own. In Jesus' Name. Amen

ACTION: Take a sheet of paper and list your plans on one side. On the other side, list God's Word about His plans.

DAY 11

IN THE MEANTIME
April 24, 2020

God will often call us to tasks that are beyond our natural ability to complete. He will also allow us to go through situations that may consume us—if not for Him being with us. Both of these scenarios are designed to cause us to draw closer to Him. He is the Source of our life—from a Creator standpoint. He *desires* to be the Source of our life—from a Father standpoint. That begins to happen when we recognize God for who He is through an intimate relationship with His Son, Jesus.

Christ calls us to take His message to the world in a variety of ways. He calls you to take His message to your world—the sphere of influence which you inhabit. But you don't have to do it alone. It's His message, so Christ provides His provision and power to proclaim and demonstrate the truth of Who He is. A wonderful result of our relationship with Jesus is that even when we feel overwhelmed by the task and the struggle, He empowers us through His Holy Spirit *every... time... we... ask!*

Even in the midst of Covid-19, take time to praise God from whom all blessings flow.

Jesus is worthy of all praise, glory and honor!

"But you will receive power when the Holy Spirit comes on you; and you will be my witnesses in Jerusalem, and in all Judea and Samaria, and to the ends of the earth." After he said this, he was taken up before their very eyes, and a cloud hid him from their sight. They were looking intently up into the sky as he was going, when suddenly two men dressed in white stood beside them. "Men of Galilee," they said, "why do you stand here looking into the sky? This same Jesus, who has been taken from you into heaven, will come back in the same way you have seen him go into heaven." -Acts 1:8-11 (NIV)

It's exciting to imagine standing on the Mount of Olives and watching Jesus fly up into the sky! But how did the disciples feel **after** He disappeared from their sight? **After** the two angels disappeared once they revealed how He will return one day in the future? How did the disciples feel as they walked back into town... alone? They now carried a major responsibility on their shoulders. They had to **continue** what Jesus had started...

The Bible says they returned with joy and worshiped Christ in the temple and prayed in an upper room together. No doubt they were excited. But in the stillness of the night, did they feel any dread, fear of the unknown or separation anxiety? Jesus spent 40 days with them *after* his resurrection, revealing to them—in ever increasing detail—the reality of the kingdom of God. No doubt, those 40 days were spectacular as they saw and heard things which blew their minds and stirred their hearts! It reminds me of when Moses spent 40 days with God on Mt. Sinai. He received amazing revelations in God's Presence. But even he had to come back down to the valley— and what a mess was waiting for him! Could it have been something similar for the disciples?

34

Have you ever felt the weight of having a monumental task on your hands which seemed beyond your ability? Perhaps you moved to a new town or started at a new school. Perhaps you were promoted at work to a position that was out of your element. Or you came home from the hospital with that new "bundle of joy" and no "instruction manual." Maybe you lost your job and didn't know how you'd take care of your family. Or you faced a major illness and the doctor's diagnosis wasn't good. Then there were the times when God impressed upon you to share His truth with someone else...

You know that feeling *we all get*, at one point or another, when we are pulled outside our comfort zones. I imagine the disciples, at some point, experienced it as well. That, **am I up for the task?** questioning. Did they feel abandoned? Did they wonder why Jesus had to go away? Why couldn't He stay? Why was He not going to free Israel from Roman oppression? And would the promised Presence of the Holy Spirit, *they had to wait for*, be everything Jesus said He would be?

I imagine at some point, maybe a day or two later reality began to set in. They were by themselves. Isn't it just like human nature to have momentary lapses between God's calling on our life and the application of God's plan? But some days later, in an upper room, the Holy Spirit ARRIVED! In that moment when God's mighty rushing wind entered them, God revealed that the disciples may have been by themselves, but they were never alone! **IN AN INSTANT**, they were filled with God's Spirit and empowered for whatever they had to face!

We have to hold out for God's **In an Instant** moments! They are the punctuation that give the sentences of our life meaning! They are the periods at the end of our struggles. They are the commas when God sees we need a break. They are the quotation marks when we desperately need a word from the

Lord. They are the exclamation points which breathe new life and strength into our souls! And they are the question marks which spur us onto the next stage of the journey. No matter how we feel in between God's calling and us carrying out that call, let us remember: *it is **God who grants us the ability to press ahead!*** It is through His indwelling Spirit that we are able to endure every struggle, while we look forward to the Day of Christ's appearing!

PRAYER: Heavenly Father, there are times when I don't feel adequate to the task You have for me to do. But You promise not only to be with me, but to also empower me through Your Holy Spirit. Help me to rely on You in everything You have given me to do. In Jesus' Name. Amen.

ACTION: Today, ask God to give you an opportunity to share Christ with someone you don't know. Trust Him to lead and guide you. Then be on the lookout!

DAY 12

JESUS: THE TRUTH TELLER

April 25, 2020

How would you describe a true friend? When I used to work at Macy's I thought one of my co-workers was a friend. One day, the regional manager came to our store for a tour. My co-worker and I were busy getting our department together. We could see the regional manager slowly making his way over. We finished with a few minutes to spare and talked face to face to be sure everything was in order.

The regional manager arrived with several others. We smiled, answered his questions, allowed him to examine our department and then he left. It seemed like a job well done! Then I took a bathroom break. To my horror, when I entered the bathroom and looked in the mirror, I saw a huge *green thing* sticking out of my nose!

After cleaning my nose (and washing my hands), I rushed back out to my co-worker and exclaimed, "I thought we were friends!" "We are," she responded. "No we are not," I replied. "Why would you say that?" she asked. "Because you didn't tell me I had a booger in my nose!" "Oh," she replied, "I didn't want to offend you." My response... "You knew it was there, didn't warn me, and let me talk to the regional manager?"

A true friend will tell you the truth. Why? Because they don't want to see you fail. Jesus is our Ultimate Friend because He loves us enough to tell us the Ultimate Truth. Why? He wants us to experience victory—in Him—for all eternity! I pray today's devotional helps you see His Truth.

Jesus is worthy of all praise, glory and honor!

24 "Therefore everyone who hears these words of mine and puts them into practice is like a wise man who built his house on the rock. 25 The rain came down, the streams rose, and the winds blew and beat against that house; yet it did not fall, because it had its foundation on the rock. 26 But everyone who hears these words of mine and does not put them into practice is like a foolish man who built his house on sand. 27 The rain came down, the streams rose, and the winds blew and beat against that house, and it fell with a great crash." - Matthew 7: 24-27 (NIV)

This passage is the summation of an entire chapter. What Jesus has said has been building up to this. He shared how we are to make judgments about others and ourselves. He shared how we are to be persistent in prayer to our Heavenly Father. He taught how we are to treat one another. He revealed that in life there are only two paths: the narrow path which leads to life and the broad path which leads to destruction. He taught how to tell the difference between a true prophet and a false one—by their fruit. And He revealed that on the day of final judgment, a genuine relationship with Him is what grants a person entrance into God's Kingdom—not their list of accomplishments apart from Him.

Jesus begins verse 24 with "Therefore." This lets us know that what is about to be said stands on the foundation of the words which came immediately before it. Here is the crux of His teaching. Here is His summation in case those who heard Him and those who would eventually read His words—us—didn't catch the central truth: **You must hear the Truth and put the Truth into practice in order to reap the benefits of the Truth.** Hearing alone is NOT enough! We must surrender our lives to what we have heard.

Jesus shares the parable about a person who *only* heard the truth and another who *both* heard and put the truth into practice. On the outside, both persons looked the same—*as long as the weather was nice.* But then the storms of life came and beat against their lives. The person who heard the truth and put it into practice was actually the one who had built their life on the strong foundation of God's rock. The other who heard, *but did not obey* had actually built their life on the sand, which provides no lasting and durable foundation at all.

Jesus lets us know that storms in life come to the Christian *and* the non-Christian. **The purpose of the storm is to reveal the true nature of the person.** We can imagine that both persons built identical houses—they sought to find fulfillment in life. They both had the same needs. But their choice of foundations were not the same. When you are looking around for God, realize He's the One supporting you! God is BIG ENOUGH to get you through ANY storm! Even this Coronavirus pandemic!

So, if you feel the ground beneath your feet being a bit unsteady, take the time NOW to build on GOD'S SURE FOUNDATION. Jesus is clear. When the storms beat against the house hard and long enough, the house built on the sand will eventually collapse. Jesus tells us ahead of time so we can make needed changes now in order to successfully endure to the end!

One thing I love about Jesus is that *He loves us enough* to tell us the TRUTH. After all... He declares in John 14:6, "I am the way and the truth and the life. No one comes to the Father except through Me."   Jesus Christ is the Rock—Our Sure Foundation upon which we stand!

PRAYER: Heavenly Father, please help me to put myself in an environment where I can hear the truth of Your Word. Then help me to put your truth into practice! In Jesus' Name. Amen.

ACTION: When you read the Bible, seek to answer these questions: Who is the writer talking to? What is the message the writer is conveying to them? How can I apply that message to my own life? Then find ways to apply the truth so you can build a strong spiritual foundation!

DAY 13

IN WAYS WE CAN'T SEE

April 26, 2020

It's been two weeks since Resurrection Sunday. Are you still here on the journey to know Christ better? Sometimes I am moved to tears when I stop and consider the immense depth of God's love for us. God saved us through His Son! He has called us into a relationship with Him that is unparalleled! No other relationship on earth can compare to knowing Jesus. And yet, we often put our other relationships before Him.

When we get to heaven, we will see that God had so much more for us to experience while on earth. Yes, we belong to Christ. Yes, we will enter His Kingdom. ***The eternity in front of us is not so much the issue. The issue is the eternity we are not fully partaking of right now: The eternity that is readily made available to every child of God—now.*** *We've all been so conditioned to view miracles as purely the Divine meeting of our* physical needs. But this is just one level of what God desires to do for us. Every miracle Jesus performs has always been to point us to an intimate relationship with the Father through Him.

May today's devotional spark a desire within you to know Jesus more intimately. May you fan that desire until it becomes a roaring flame. Eternal life is knowing the Father and Jesus Christ whom He has sent (John 17:3).

Jesus is worthy of all the praise, glory and honor!

"I am the vine; you are the branches. If you remain in me and I in you, you will bear much fruit; apart from me you can do nothing." - John 15:5 (NIV)

When Jesus said this, did He *REALLY* mean we could do *NOTHING* without him? Or was He just being a *bit* dramatic? Well, Jesus was **never** dramatic simply for the sake of being so. Everything He did and said always had a purpose. He also never minced words. He meant what He said and He said what He meant. No one spoke truth to power more than He did! So, if Jesus wasn't exaggerating, then what could He possibly mean when He said, "Without Me you can do nothing"?

The context of His statement was Him being the vine and we being the branches *which connect to* the vine. Just as a branch has no life in it apart from being connected to the vine, *we also have no life in us apart from being connected to Him.* He is *CENTRAL*. We are *secondary*. If a branch is severed from the vine, it immediately begins to lose its life and soon dies. If we live severed from Christ, then we are in the process of losing life. Does this mean everyone on earth living without giving Jesus a second thought are really the "walking dead?" Yes. *Even though we are busy doing things, chasing ambitions and reaching goals,* **without Christ our work and our life adds up to nothing when placed next to eternity.**

The late Christian apologist, Ravi Zacharias states, *"Jesus didn't come to make bad people good. He came to make dead people live!"* Jesus offers those of us who will receive Him an entirely *new* way to live—a different category of *existence*.

Scripture teaches that Jesus created the universe. By Him all things are held together (Colossians 1:16-17). So, that means *quite literally, without Jesus we could do nothing.* Why? Because if He holds everything together, then without Him our lives would fall apart and we would cease to exist. He is holding us together in ways we can't even comprehend!

On the day of Judgment, there will be no self-made men and women standing before God claiming their own greatness. On that day, *we all will see* that even in our rebellion, Jesus literally held our existence together by the word of His power (Hebrews 1:3). So, no one will be able to claim that He didn't love them. No one will be able to say that God didn't care. No one will be able to say that God wasn't present in the midst of trying situations. For the One who is the Source of all life, the First and the Last, Who was dead but now is alive forevermore emphatically declares: *"Without Me you can do nothing."*

If Christ does this for all of us—even those who refuse to surrender and acknowledge Him as Lord and Savior of their life, then imagine what He will do for those who *do* surrender to Him! He invites us to move from the formality of merely seeing God as Creator, to intimately knowing God as our Sustainer! That is such a sweet relationship... being in communion with The Father and The Son through the Holy Spirit every day of our lives: knowing that this communion will last into eternity. It is out of this intimacy with Christ—as a branch stays connected to the vine—that we begin to bring forth true fruit in life. Fruit that brings honor to God's Kingdom.

If God never does another thing for you, He *has* already *and is* already doing all that needs to be done through His Son, Jesus. Truly, without Him, you and I can do nothing!

PRAYER: Heavenly Father, open my eyes to the ways You provide for me that I usually don't pay attention to. In Jesus' Name. Amen.

ACTION: Make a list of all the ways God provides for you.

DAY 14

THE HEART OF OUR FATHER

April 27, 2020

Have you ever wondered why people become enemies?

Sometimes it's because of **misinformation**: someone was told incorrect details about another. Sometimes it's because of **misunderstanding**: someone heard what the other said, but received the message differently from how it was intended. Sometimes it's because of **arrogance**: a person thinks they are better than another and don't want to see them thrive in life. Sometimes it's because of **insecurity**: a person doesn't like that the other seems more confident than they are. Sometimes it's because of **projecting**: a person sees another who reminds them of someone else who hurt them in the past.

There are more reasons why people become enemies— reasons we don't have time to address here. But Jesus Christ demonstrates through His teachings and His living how those who follow Him are called to treat their enemies. When we examine His example, we are left with a two-part question: Are we busy trying to justify why we hate our enemies? Or are we seeking the heart of our Father Who loves them just as much as He loves us? Hopefully, today's devotional will help us find some clarity.

Jesus is worthy of all the praise, glory and honor!

43 "You have heard that it was said, ' Love your neighbor and hate your enemy.' 44 But I tell you, love your enemies and pray for those who persecute you, 45 that you may be children of your Father in heaven. He causes his sun to rise on the evil and the good, and sends rain on the righteous and the unrighteous." -Matthew 5:43-45 (NIV)

This command from Jesus makes no sense to us if we neglect the reality of His resurrection. "Why should I love someone who is trying to harm me? Why should I love someone who is trying to manipulate and deceive me? Why should I pray for someone who doesn't like me and may be trying to kill me?" Jesus' resurrection life answers these questions and more...

First, Jesus' life bears witness to the fact that the person standing in front of you—*your enemy*—does not have to remain your enemy. The tremendous love of Jesus flowing through you has the potential to change them. Jesus rose from the dead with power over our **REAL enemy: Satan**. The person who stands in opposition to you is really being manipulated by the <u>real enemy of **all** of our souls</u>. The truth is, if *we* don't realize this, we too can be manipulated if we continue to hold grudges. Jesus desires for all of us to be free!

Second, Jesus says how we treat our enemies indicates the strength of our relationship with our Heavenly Father. Children usually want to do what their parents do. They want to please them. Our Heavenly Father loved humanity so much that He sent Jesus to redeem us. As His children, He desires us to be like Him in our love for others. Through His death and resurrection, Jesus came to enemies and made them friends. As our "Big Brother," He has set the standard for us to follow.

Third, Jesus says our Heavenly Father showers blessings on the saved and the unsaved. Why? Because He knows how much the true enemy—Satan—has corrupted us through sin. So, God extends mercy to all so we can experience His love. Even with our many problems, no one will be able to accuse God of not caring about our struggles! God extends a common grace to all and a particular grace to His redeemed. As His children, we have access to His redemptive love through Christ which can help set our enemies free from enslavement to the devil—who the Bible calls the Accuser, Liar, Thief, Destroyer, and the one who deceives the whole world!

Lastly, since God loves humanity enough to create the way for those who receive His Son to escape the wrath laid up for Satan and his fallen angels—*do you* have enough love in your heart to desire the salvation of your enemies? Or would you rather see them burn in hell? If you want to hate somebody, hate the devil and the demons! **Ephesians 6 tells us that our *real battle* is with them.** Don't allow the attacks of another human being cause you to desire their ultimate destruction. Yes, everyone will not be saved. Yes, people must pay the consequence for their sinful actions. But as children of God, our calling is to demonstrate the love of Christ to people—especially our enemies—while they still have time to repent.

As followers of Jesus Christ we are free to love our enemies! Free to love those who mistreat us! Yes, their attacks on us are painful. Jesus is not denying this fact. The truth is He experienced more pain at the hands of His enemies than we will experience at the hands of ours. Yet, He was able to say, "Father forgive them for they don't know what they are doing." Jesus is not commanding us to do what He hasn't already done. He wants us to keep our eyes on the bigger picture. We can only do this by surrendering to God's love. When we look at things through the light of Christ's resurrection, everything will begin to change. What we once found impossible to do will become possible and we will see ourselves as God sees and desires us to be: ministers of reconciliation! (2 Corinthians 5:11-21)

PRAYER: Heavenly Father, please give me Your heart for my enemies. Help me to see, know and act in a way that will help draw them to You. In Jesus' Name. Amen.

ACTION: Make a list of your enemies. Begin to pray that God would bless them, save them and turn them into friends. Ask God to search your heart and expose any attitude or action that may be contributing to the problem—so you can repent. Be ready to take any action the Lord reveals to you to help bring reconciliation.

DAY 15

THE PROOF OF LOVE
April 28, 2020

We see many Covid-19 survivors showing gratitude to the nurses and doctors who helped save their lives. They have acknowledged, in the most public of ways, their thanks to these medical professionals who have put their lives on the line to save others. It's been heartwarming to see their public displays of affection: videos, cards, food, gifts, hugs, and tears... No doubt, if the doctors or nurses ever needed their former patients, they would drop everything to help. Why? Because these survivors wouldn't be alive if it weren't for these first responders.

Jesus is our Ultimate First Responder! Just like doctors and nurses are leaving their homes and families to help patients, Jesus left Heaven and came to earth to carry out His Father's mission: the salvation of humanity. You see, our hearts were infected and corrupted by SIN—the worst virus known to man. SIN has taken and continues to take the lives of untold billions —with devastating effects. But Jesus came with the vaccine: His blood. He sacrificed His life on the cross and rose from the dead so those who believe in Him could be set free. With a love like this who wouldn't want to express their *eternal* gratitude by pledging their allegiance to Jesus?

Jesus is worthy of all praise, glory and honor!

"If you love Me, keep my commands." -John 14:15 (NIV)

The first step after receiving Christ *as Savior* is to learn about His life, teachings and commands. The second step is to actually *obey* His commands. It is through this ongoing process that Jesus *becomes our Lord*. A problem is that many Christians don't know what Jesus commands! Sure we've heard, *treat others like you want to be treated* and *turn the other cheek,* but even here we are often disobedient. Do we take Jesus seriously when He ties our *love for Him* directly to our *obedience to Him?*

Isn't that like the relationship between a parent and a child? A child cannot proclaim love for the parent while *always* being disobedient. It's one thing to misunderstand the command, but it's another to rebel against or disregard it. Also, ignorance of a command may get a child out of trouble the first time, but once the parent establishes that the child *knows what is expected*, the child is now held accountable.

The question is: **Do we see ourselves as children of God?** If we belong to Jesus, then that is who we are. God is our Heavenly Father. Christ is our Savior and Lord Who speaks on behalf of His Father. To obey Christ is to obey the Father because they are one and are always in agreement with one another. So, Jesus makes a clear statement that has no room for misunderstanding: *"If you love Me, keep My commands."* Jesus ties our verbal "I love you Lord" with the actions of our mind and body. What Jesus is getting at is **the condition and leaning of our heart.**

We have no problems submitting ourselves to the people and things which truly *capture* our heart. Think about couples who spend all of their time together; who finish each other's sentences and have taken on one another's traits! Or the person who has a favorite hobby and can spend all day doing that "thing." They can work right through lunch and dinner without missing a beat. And they can talk about their hobby with anyone who's interested and never grow tired of the conversation! In both of these cases, the people's hearts have been *captured*. And Jesus says in Matthew 6:21, *"For where your treasure is, there your heart will be also."*

Is Jesus your treasure? Has He *captured* your heart? Or are other things in the way? Do you desire to know everything about Him? Do you know how He feels about situations — based on His teachings? If you don't understand Him, ask Him to open your mind *(Luke 24:45)*. If you feel His commands are too hard, ask Him for the faith, strength and endurance to carry them out *(Luke 17:5)*! Ask Him to let His life course through your veins so it's actually Him empowering you with the desire and ability to obey *(John 6:63)*. Be honest about the times you don't *feel* like doing God's Will and ask for His Help once more to obey *(Luke 22:42)*.

Jesus knows all things. He never acts out of fear and insecurity. His expectations are never unrealistic. His thoughts and actions are always morally right and true. We can count on Him wanting what's best for us, even if what is *best* is extremely difficult. If we knew just how much He *loved* us, we would obey His commands. So, let's take time to study His Word so we can know His *heart* for those who are called to follow Him. Do you love Him?

PRAYER: Heavenly Father, help me to be obedient to the commands You give through Christ Your Son. Thank You for Your grace and mercy. In Jesus' Name. Amen.

ACTION: Search the Scriptures and make a list of Jesus' commands. Then seek to follow them.

DAY 16

FOLLOWING DIRECTIONS

April 29, 2020

Sometimes it's hard to follow someone when you don't know where they are going. The last couple of nice days, my son and I went for a walk (while wearing our masks and practicing social distancing). While he was excited to get out of the apartment, he was curious to know where we were going. I gave him the general route, but didn't tell him every specific street. Why? Because he didn't need to know.

He was fine with the direction until half way through the walk. He wanted to turn down a familiar road to head back. I told him to take a different path. He hesitated, but obeyed. As we walked through an area *he was unfamiliar with*, he asked: "Daddy. Do you know where we are going? Have you gone this way before?" I assured him I knew the area. After a while, he began to trust my words and continued to enjoy the walk. We had a wonderful time and made it home just fine.

As you walk with Jesus, there will be times He will lead you down unfamiliar roads. You don't have to worry. He knows where He is going and He will get you home just fine.

Jesus is worthy of all the praise, glory and honor!

"That day when evening came, he said to his disciples, "Let us go over to the other side." -Mark 4:35 (NIV)

Jesus never sends you where He isn't willing to go. In fact, Psalm 23 states, "The LORD is my Shepherd, I shall not want." A shepherd not only goes *with* the sheep... He also goes *before* the sheep and scouts out the path which they are to take. So, Jesus tells His disciples, *"Let us go over to the other side,"* and they get in a boat and make their way across the massive lake which spanned more than 8 miles across.

Jesus is so exhausted He snuggles up to a cushion and quickly falls asleep in the corner of the boat. Moments later, a furious storm breaks out over the lake! Suddenly, the moon and stars in the sky are blocked by thick clouds, as wind kicks up the waves! The boat rocks back and forth. Water splashes over the sides! The men, many who had made their living on boats, become terrified and wake the Master.

The disciples cried out, "Teacher, don't you care if we drown?" Their plea shows their battle with unbelief. **Of course** Jesus cares if they drown! After all, He's the one who called them to follow Him! He's the one who has been teaching them about the truths of God's Kingdom. He's the one who has been providing for them. And... He's in the boat *with them!* But they have lost sight of the bigger picture: they are *with Jesus* on a mission. Jesus has to carry out the will of His Father. Do you think a mere storm can stop God's plan from happening?

Jesus got up and rebuked the wind and the waves. *"Peace, be still!"* The very elements of nature responded to His command. In an instant, everything was calm and the boat steadied on the smooth waters. The clouds rolled back and the starry sky twinkled once again. In the moonlight, Jesus turned to His followers and asked them a pointed question. **"Why are you so afraid? Do you still have no faith?"** In essence, Jesus is asking them, *"Have you not yet learned how to place your faith in Me?"*

Notice, they didn't wake Jesus up as soon as the storm hits. They called on Him in desperation as a last ditch effort! **They wondered**, *how in the world could He be sleep during the storm?* **And Jesus wondered**, _how in the world could they still have issues trusting Me after everything they've seen Me do?_ The disciples meet His questions with an awed silence before saying to one another, "What kind of man is this? Even the wind and waves obey Him!"

We've all gone through storms in life and felt like we were alone. We saw the large waves and felt the raging wind gusts. We were, in fact sinking. We did everything we could in our own strength and nothing changed. We cried out, "God where are You? Don't You care that I'm drowning?!" God, in His mercy, brought us *through* that situation. Going forward though, **we need to know that if we belong to Christ, then He is with us in the boat of our life—waiting for us to call on Him.** So, there is no need to be afraid. Fear clouds our view of God's Presence.

With everything we have experienced *with Jesus*, why do we still struggle to have faith? Jesus desires to show us, as He did His disciples, just how powerful His Resurrection Life can be to those who believe. If we are with Jesus and He is with us, then no storm can derail God's plan and purpose for our life! The King of Kings is in our boat; and we must follow Him wherever He goes!

PRAYER: Heavenly Father, help me to trust that You know where You are taking me. Please build up faith within me. My life is in Your most capable hands! In Jesus' Name. Amen.

ACTION: When Jesus leads you to take an unfamiliar route in life, give Him your fear and uncertainty, ask for His courage and obey His command.

DAY 17

FROM DIRECTION TO DESTINATION
April 30, 2020

Sometimes we can be so focused on the destination that we miss the journey. Other times, we are so focused on the journey that we miss the destination. The Christian life is about being so focused on our Shepherd, that we become full participants in the journey *and* the destination—because Jesus fully participates in both. As we follow Christ, He not only leads us through a variety of terrains, but He also brings us into the presence of a variety of people. He does all of this for the glory of His Heavenly Father.

What is the glory of His Heavenly Father? *"He has rescued us from the dominion of darkness and brought us into the kingdom of His beloved Son, 14 in whom we have redemption, the forgiveness of sins"* (Colossians 1:13-14). As you journey through life, you will discover some directions and destinations that are not on your map. Don't worry, Jesus has them on His. It is in those times and places where He builds your faith so you can be of service to Him. Seek to follow where He leads and to do what He commands and you will see the glory of the Father displayed in your midst!

Jesus is worthy of all praise, glory and honor!

"Then Jesus asked him, 'What is your name?'" Mark 5:9 (NIV)

In our last devotional, we looked at Mark 4:35 where Jesus told His disciples to go to the other side of the lake. He fell asleep in the boat; then a sudden storm arose. The terrified disciples woke Jesus up! He rebuked the storm… *and them.* "Why are you so afraid?" He asked. "Do you still have no faith?" The main message of the devotional was: <u>if we belong to Christ, then He is with us in the boat of our life—waiting for us to call on Him. So there is no need to be afraid.</u> I hope you take this to heart. Today's devotional continues to build on this line of thought.

While Jesus gave the direction, He did not tell His disciples where they were going. This might come as a surprise… but if you read Mark 4:35 to Mark 5:20 you will discover that <u>the storm wasn't even about the disciples</u>—*at least not directly.* Jesus was on a mission to free a man who was hopelessly bound by evil spirits. It can be inferred from the story that the source of the storm was demonic in nature. It was a preemptive attack to stop Jesus from arriving at the tombs where a tortured man lived in constant agony.

But Jesus could not be stopped! He confronted the man and asked for his name. The demons took over the man's vocal cords and replied: calling themselves *Legion.* In the Roman army, a legion of soldiers numbered between 3,000 to 6,000 men! *This man* was so empowered by demons that his ferociousness could not be tamed! When men tied him up with ropes and metal chains—in an attempt to subdue him—he easily broke their restraints! All persons in that area feared this man and kept their distance. The chaos within his soul splintered his mind so, that he cut himself with sharp stones and yelled at the top of his lungs day and night!

The Bible doesn't tell us how long he had been in this state of demonic oppression. Nor does it say how he became possessed. But it does reveal that on this particular night Jesus arrived at the tombs—on mission—ready to do battle. No doubt, the demons tried to resist, but with a word they were cast out of the man. They entered a herd of nearby pigs and immediately caused their deaths. Moments later, the man was in his right frame of mind—free from oppression—ready to follow Jesus… Word spread quickly and the people from the surrounding areas were amazed!

I wonder how the disciples felt as they watched this scene play out before their eyes? They could not have imagined what was waiting on the other side of the lake. If they could, they probably would not have gone. In the midst of the storm, they forgot it was Jesus who gave the command in the first place. So, when the unexpected storm raged against their boat, the disciples thought it was all about them. "Teacher, don't you care if **WE** drown?" But it wasn't about them! *It was about Christ and His mission*. *And they were there to serve Him as He carried out His mission*. They didn't realize He didn't just give the command because He had nothing else better to do. Jesus *always* has a purpose in what He does.

When you face a storm in life, don't automatically assume it's about you. Stop and ask God what the purpose is. Ask for the ability to discern God's Will in that particular moment. Ask for His vantage point. You may just discover that it's not about you, but about someone else needing freedom. You are, after all, following the Shepherd who leaves the ninety-nine to go and save the one. Jesus continues to be about His Father's business. He continues His mission to set the captives free from the oppression of the enemy. And He will often include you and me in His battle plans. May we—while there is still time—live in service to our King as He continues to seek and save the lost (Luke 19:10). Amen.

PRAYER: Heavenly Father, in every situation please help me to see Christ and His mission. And may I act accordingly. In Jesus' Name. Amen.

ACTION: Look for opportunities to be used by Jesus to help set someone else free from oppression.

DAY 18

TO WHOM SHALL WE GO?

May 1, 2020

What's more important to you? God meeting your physical need or God saving your soul and giving your life purpose? Why am I raising these questions? Because people will often give up on their pursuit of God when He doesn't meet their physical needs. I've heard so many stories where people have abandoned God because their bills weren't paid, or they lost a job or a loved one got sick and died. Please don't let this be you! I want to see you win the race that God has placed in front of you! I want to see you in heaven and on the new earth after Christ returns and vanquishes evil forever!

Jesus promises to meet our needs as our hearts and minds are centered on Him and His Kingdom. ***Understand though, that our greatest need is to know Him.*** <u>The TRUTH is, if God never does another thing for us, He has already given us everything we need through the life, death, burial and resurrection of His Son!</u> There are times when God refuses to meet a physical need in order to meet our deeper spiritual need: Understanding Who Christ **IS**. So, when God chooses to "talk" instead of "perform," try not to get mad or frustrated. Trust that God knows what He's doing; that He knows you better than you know yourself; and that He will work all things out for His glory and your good.

Jesus is worthy of all praise, glory and honor!

66 "From this time many of His disciples turned back and no longer followed Him. 67 'You do not want to leave too, do you?' Jesus asked the twelve. 68 Simon Peter answered Him, 'Lord, to whom shall we go? You have the words of eternal life. 69 We have come to believe and to know that You are the Holy One of God.'" -John 6:66-69 (NIV)

Have you ever heard someone say, "I'll believe it when I see it." You know, that is not always true. One day, a crowd of 5,000+ people had been following Jesus because of His healing miracles. He took a boy's bag lunch, blessed and multiplied its contents and fed the people until they were full. The disciples gathered up 12 baskets of leftovers! The people declared Jesus to be a prophet. Talk about God making a way out of no way!

But Jesus withdrew from the crowd and found a private place to pray. That windy night the 12 disciples got in a boat to cross the Sea of Galilee's choppy waters. About 4 miles into their journey, they saw Jesus walking towards them on the waves! They were shocked, amazed and frightened at the same time! The next day, some of the crowd got in boats and crossed the water in search of Jesus. They found Him on the other side and hoped He would do more miracles to meet their needs.

But Jesus began teaching them. Some sayings they found hard to receive. Here's a few things He said: *"I am the Bread of life. The one who comes to Me will never be hungry, and the one who believes in Me will never be thirsty" (vs.35)*. He also said, *"For I have come down from heaven, not to do My own will, but to do the will of Him who sent Me" (vs.38)*. Then there was this, *"I am the Living Bread that came down out of heaven. If anyone eats of this Bread, he will live forever. And the Bread that I will give for the life of the world is My flesh" (vs.51)*. And also this, *"The one who eats My flesh and drinks My blood has eternal life, and I will raise him up on the last day"* (vs.55).

The people grumbled amongst themselves. They found His words harsh and offensive. "Who does Jesus think He is? How could He come from heaven? We know His parents! How can He give us His flesh to eat?" As a result, the crowd abandoned Him. **All of the *"I'll believe it when I see it"* people were gone...** Only the twelve were left.

Jesus didn't chase after the crowd. In fact, He watched them leave. I'm sure He was disappointed, but He stayed on mission —knowing there would be those who believed and those who would not. After watching the "exodus," He turned to His twelve and asked a serious question: ***"You do not want to leave too, do you?"*** Can you imagine the look in His eyes and the inflection in His voice? Peter replied, *"Lord, to whom shall we go? You alone have the words of eternal life."*

People who only live for "signs" will never follow Jesus all the way. Why? Because they are "**ME**" focused. *What's in it for me, Jesus? How can I get my needs met?* Yes, Jesus **does** *give signs*, but the purpose is **always** to point us to the love of His Father in heaven. The primary way Jesus points us to His Father (outside of the cross) is by teaching us the TRUTH. Jesus gave the people TRUTH and they didn't like it because it forced them to realize they were not the center of existence— *JESUS IS!*

I like Peter's two-part reply (vs. 68-69) on behalf of the twelve: *"Lord, to whom shall we go?"* He knows **to leave Jesus is to go and follow someone else**—whether it's self, family, friends, or the devil. Peter is saying, no one is more important than Jesus. Then he adds, *"You have the words of eternal life. We have come to believe and to know that You are the Holy*

One of God." It is their receiving of signs **and** teaching *together* which has enabled them to believe that Jesus truly is the Messiah!

Don't let the hard teachings of Jesus turn you away. They are invitations for you to draw near to Him for understanding. His greatest sign was and is His death on the cross and His resurrection from the dead. Only the hungry will feed on the Bread of heaven and be satisfied.

PRAYER: Heavenly Father, help me to see and know that Christ alone has the words of eternal life. Help me to believe and know that He is Your Holy One. In Jesus' Name. Amen.

ACTION: Make a concerted effort to gather a small group together to study the teachings of Jesus.

DAY 19

LIFE HIMSELF

May 2, 2020

With so many people dying around us, it's good to be reminded that one day our current pain will become a distant memory. RESURRECTION IS COMING! The Greek word for "resurrection" is *Anastasis*. It means: *rising to life; returning to life after death, usually referring to the raising to life of Jesus Christ.* As you will read in today's devotional, what is true of Christ—that He rose from the dead—will be true of us. We and our loved ones who have died in Christ, will be raised as well.

If I may share a quote from my previous book: *"Resurrection is a bursting forth! It is where God supernaturally infuses His abundant, overflowing and unquenchable Holy Spirit through the very atoms that make up your body; through the very substance of nature and spirit, which makes up the totality of who you are... Where God reverses what is otherwise irreversible... It is not only restoring what was lost, it is also bestowing upon us what we never had."*

The eternal life God has planned for us through His Son is and will be unimaginably spectacular *(1 Corinthians 2:9)*! The Bible reminds us in the midst of death, that as Christ-followers, we are to encourage each other with this truth *(1 Thessalonians 4:18)*.

Note: *The above quote is from, Resurrection: The BIG Picture of God's Purpose and Your Destiny.*

Jesus is worthy of all praise, glory and honor!

25 "Jesus said to her, 'I am the resurrection and the life. The one who believes in Me will live, even though they die; 26 And whoever lives by believing in Me will never die. Do you believe this?' 27 'Yes, Lord,' she replied, "I believe that You are the Messiah, the Son of God, who is to come into the world.'" - John 11:25-27 (NIV)

Lazarus was dead. His sisters, Mary and Martha, were devastated. Jesus could have gotten to them earlier, when He first received word that Lazarus was sick, but He didn't come. It wasn't that Jesus couldn't—*but that He would not.* Even though, He loved Lazarus like a brother, He still had to obey His Father's Will. In this case, His Father's will was for Lazarus to die, knowing his family and friends would be distraught, and then for Jesus to come and perform the greatest miracle they all had seen up to that point: *raising Lazarus after he had been dead four days.*

This is significant. The Pharisees made plans to kill Lazarus because his resurrection caused many to place their faith in Jesus (John 12:10). But why was this miracle unique from the other times Jesus raised people from the dead? Jewish thought was that after a person died, their spirit remained nearby for up to 3 days. Within that time, a miracle *could be possible*. However, after the 3rd day, the person's spirit would depart into the afterlife and the dead body would begin undergoing advanced stages of decay. In the Jewish mind, resurrection after 3 days was impossible—except by God Himself. So, Jesus raising Lazarus from the dead after he had been dead 4 days, was irrefutable proof that He was the Messiah! *(And yet some still refused to believe...)*

Jesus returned to Bethany and Martha said to Him, *"Lord, if you had been here, my brother would not have died. But I know that even now God will give you whatever you ask"* (vs.

21-22). What happens next is one of the most profound conversations on spiritual reality, since Jesus spoke with Nicodemus by night and sat with the woman at the well. Jesus told Martha that her brother would rise again. She agreed that he would, at the resurrection on the last day when God judges the world. THEN Jesus declared, *"I am the resurrection and the life. The one who believes in Me will live even though they die; and whoever lives by believing in Me will never die. Do you believe this?"*

Jesus *doesn't just have* the power of resurrection. He *doesn't just have* the power of life. Jesus **IS** RESURRECTION LIFE! He **IS** the SOURCE of RESURRECTION LIFE! To be in relationship with Jesus is to be in relationship with life itself… or rather **Life Himself**. When Jesus raised Lazarus from the dead, He didn't just call Lazarus' soul back into his body. If that was all, then Lazarus would have been like the zombies on the Walking Dead TV show. Remember when they rolled the stone away? Lazarus' body was so decayed that the stench was unbearable! But Jesus, being **Life Himself**, completely reversed death! He healed a decayed body—making it brand new—AND THEN called Lazarus' soul back within it!

There's something else… Jesus said. *"The one who believes in Me will live even though they die; and whoever lives by believing in Me will never die."* On the surface, this seems like an oxymoron or at least a conundrum. However, Jesus is talking about two very different kinds of death here. The word "die" in the Greek is "apothnēskō and it has several contextual meanings. If we replace "die" with the appropriate meaning, this is what we get: *"The one who believes in Me will live even though they **will physically die one day**; and whoever lives by believing in Me will never **have to face eternal death and be subject to eternal misery in hell.**"* Revelation 20:14 refers to this eternal death and misery in hell as "the second death." In fact, "the second death," which is called the lake of fire is worse than hell. In verses 14 and 15 we read: *"Then death and Hades were thrown into the lake of fire. The lake of fire is the second death." 15 Anyone whose name was not found written in the book of life was thrown into the lake of fire."*

We all will experience "the first death," but only those who don't believe in Christ will experience "the second death." Although Jesus raised Lazarus back to life, eventually he died again. But Jesus had *EVEN GREATER PROOF* that He was truly the Messiah: He Himself suffered and died in our place, was buried in a borrowed tomb, and rose back to life on the third day—**NEVER TO DIE AGAIN!** And Jesus reveals the decree of His Father in John 6:39-40: that we who belong to Christ will be raised to eternal life on the last day. Revelation 20:6 also reveals that "the second death" has no power over those who belong to Christ. That makes perfect sense. For we are in relationship with He Who **IS** the RESURRECTION and THE LIFE. We may, like Lazarus' family and friends, weep *now*, but on *the last day* we will celebrate God's sovereign goodness with Lazarus, Mary, Martha and an innumerable number of sisters and brothers in Christ Jesus. Hallelujah! Amen!

PRAYER: Heavenly Father, please help me to understand the reality of Christ's resurrection and how it changes everything. In Jesus' Name. Amen.

ACTION: Take time to study Jesus' words to Martha and Mary. Make time to meditate on them and what it ultimately means for you and those who know Christ.

DAY 20

GOD'S GOT YOU!
May 3, 2020

It's so easy to worry about things. I won't even list them because you already know what you worry about. However, Jesus tells us not to worry about *anything*, but rather He invites us to learn how to trust God in *everything*. And guess what? There's no "small print" in Jesus' command that reads, *"worrying is applicable in certain situations where we feel the situation is too big for God to handle—such as plagues, medical conditions, bills, unmet expectations, etc…"*

Learning *not* to worry is a process. So is learning to *trust* God. Both are two sides of the same coin called, *spiritual maturity*. As we grow in our relationship with God, our ability to trust Him grows too—and our worrying decreases. Today's devotional is a reminder of this truth. So, be encouraged!

Jesus is worthy of all praise, glory and honor!

"Therefore do not worry about tomorrow, for tomorrow will worry about itself. Each day has enough trouble of its own." - Matthew 6:34 (NIV)

Last August, my wife and I took our 8 year old son on a surprise trip to Florida. He had no idea where we were going until we got to the airport. As the trip unfolded, he didn't know what we would be doing. ***But we did.*** We planned the entire trip: Disney, Universal Studios, Bethune-Cookman University (my alma mater), and visiting relatives. We had fun, educational opportunities and intimate family bonding time. Ultimately, we had one goal for our son: <u>Don't worry about anything. Just be a kid and enjoy the trip.</u>

Did he do that? Not really. Sure he had pockets of time where he truly enjoyed himself and laughed and sang and danced and hopped and did everything else an 8 year old boy would do (like make silly noises). *<u>But there were times when he was overly concerned about what would come next.</u>* What would happen later. What would take place tomorrow. Would there be enough time and did we have enough resources to do what he wanted to do? At times, this concern consumed his thoughts and caused him to miss the beauty of what he was currently experiencing in the moment.

We assured our son that he need not worry. Mommy and daddy had planned for every aspect of this trip. He was free to enjoy himself, us and the journey. And when he had concerns, he could bring them to us and we would take care of them or show him how to handle them. So, he was free to be a kid. He didn't have to worry about a thing. He could focus on having fun (within our parameters), learning new things and being obedient to what we told him to do.

You know, our relationship with God is similar to the dynamics of this Florida trip. **Our Heavenly Father wants us to just be His kids, through Christ Jesus, and not worry about anything.** Jesus tells us that our Heavenly Father already knows what we need (vs.32). Then He tells us that the orienting factor of our life should be to seek His kingdom and His righteousness—**_first_** (vs. 33). In other words, Christ tells us that when our heart's desire is to live for Him, then our Heavenly Father will make sure that we have everything we need to live.

There's a difference between *acknowledging* that we have a need and being *worried* about our needs. God wants us to come to Him with our needs, but He doesn't want us to be consumed by them. Worrying means: *to be anxious, to be troubled with cares, to seek to promote one's interests*. When we worry, we are in fact saying to God, "I don't trust that You can handle this situation. I can't see how You are going to work things out. I need to take my own interests into my own hands." **But worrying adds nothing to our lives!** *It actually steals from us:* our peace of mind, our physical health, our spiritual faith reserves, our ability to have strong relationships with the people we care about, our sense of community, and it clogs our lines of communication with God.

God has planned out every aspect of our trip on earth. (Ephesians 2:10) We can focus on having fun—*(the Lord's way),* learning new things and taking care of responsibilities, all while *being obedient* to His Word, His leading and His love. The question is: Will we trust Christ for each day or will we worry about tomorrow? Jesus tells us not to be consumed with anxiety for tomorrow. When we do, we miss the opportunities and blessings of today. So, what should we do? Philippians 4:6-7 tells us: 6*"Do not be anxious about anything, but in every situation, by prayer and petition, with thanksgiving, present your requests to God. 7 And the peace of God, which transcends all understanding, will guard your hearts and your minds in Christ Jesus."*

PRAYER: Heavenly Father, thank you for taking care of me every second of every day. Help me to not be consumed with anxiety for today nor tomorrow. Help me to not stress over anything and just enjoy being Your kid. In Jesus' Name. Amen.

ACTION: List every prayer God has answered and thank Him for His faithfulness.

DAY 21

REPRESENTATIVES OF JESUS

May 4, 2020

I remember when Michael Jackson died. I was at Best Buy on Fordham Road in the Bronx. While perusing the movie section, a man—whom I did not know—walked right up to me and said, "Did you hear? Michael Jackson just died." We talked for a few minutes before I left to catch my train. At the station, everyone was in shock. We were all strangers—talking to each other about a man who had impacted our lives—even though we had never met him.

As Christians, you and I follow a Man who died. The difference between His death and MJ's is that Jesus died to redeem and save humanity. Michael's death did nothing but remind us that if the King of Pop could die, so will we one day. As Christ-followers, the story of Jesus' redemptive death is only the beginning. Because three days later, the KING of Kings and LORD of Lords rose from the dead with all power in His hands! And because of His death and resurrection, all who believe can be saved for eternity.

Are we willing and able to walk up to perfect strangers and tell them THIS Good News?

Jesus is worthy of all praise, glory and honor!

"But you shall receive power, after that the Holy Spirit has come upon you; and you shall be witnesses to me in Jerusalem, and in all Judea and Samaria, and to the end of the earth." -Acts 1:8 (NKJV)

We are witnesses all the time. We continually tell others what we have seen, heard and experienced. We share what we love. If we've watched an amazing show—be it on Broadway, on television, or at the movies—we will scream it from the rooftops! We will post about it on social media. We will mention it to strangers on the bus, train, and airplane. We also share what we don't like. If we've had a bad experience—like encountering a racist clerk while shopping or Starbucks running out of coffee—we will also tell everyone we know through the same methods of communication. In short, we are witnesses whether we notice it or not. But, **When it comes to Jesus are we His witnesses?**

Jesus told His disciples that they would be **witnesses to Him**. They would represent to others what they have seen, heard and experienced with Christ. They would share His truth, revelation and love. They would learn to be more concerned with how Christ saw them than how the world *they were sent into* thought of them. As *witnesses to Jesus*, they would be light and salt in a dark decaying world: reflecting His Light to others and preserving lives from spoiling. How Jesus called them is also how He calls us.

But, if we are honest, sometimes it's easier to be witnesses to the things of the world than it is to the things of Heaven. Have you ever asked yourself why this is the case? Why is it so easy to talk about things which don't matter once we step into eternity, but we are silent on the One Thing that matters forever? There are at least two reasons.

ONE: The Bible refers to the internal battle which rages within each of us: the battle between our flesh (sinful nature) and our spirit. Our spirit wants to please God, but our flesh wants to please self (Romans 7:14-25). That's why, even when the Holy Spirit compels us, we hesitate or outright refuse to share Christ with others in our daily lives. If we are not aware of the battle, then we won't call on God for reinforcements so we can accomplish His will.

TWO: The Bible also tells us that Satan's empire actively tries to resist God's Kingdom (Ephesians 6:10-20). 2 Corinthians 4:4 says that Satan is the "god of this world" who blinds the minds of unbelievers. He is also called the "prince and power of the air" who works in the hearts and minds of those who rebel against God (Ephesians 2:2). So, when the enemy sees that we seek to share Jesus with those he oppresses, the enemy fights our attempts. Being unaware of this battle, causes us to succumb to illegitimate thoughts of fear and timidity the devil tries to plant in our minds.

We must remind ourselves to Whom we belong! Jesus calls us to be *witnesses to Him*. We are His ambassadors, calling the dead to be reconciled to God through Christ so they can live (2 Corinthians 5:17-21). There's one more aspect to being a *witness to Jesus*. "Witness," in the Greek, is **martyrs**. It's where we get the word *martyr: someone who undergoes a violent death while demonstrating their faith in Jesus Christ.* Being a *witness to Jesus* means we trust His plan for our life; knowing He can even use our death to draw the lost to Himself. As *witnesses to Jesus*, no experience is wasted.

PRAYER: Heavenly Father, please help me to be Your representative here on earth. May I no longer be a witness to the things of the world more than being a witness to the realty of heaven. In Jesus' Name. Amen.

ACTION: Make a rule... for every time you share a favorite show, song or hobby with someone, that week you have to share a Scripture verse, devotional, biblical insight or prayer with someone as well.

DAY 22

ARE YOU DRINKING LIVING WATER?

May 5, 2020

God has provisions laid up for us as His children. He has resources we don't even know about. According to 2 Peter 1:1-4, all of these resources, provisions and promises are found in Jesus Christ Himself. As we walk day-by-day let us remember that God not only has what we need, but HE IS WHO WE NEED. The One who provides is always greater than the provision that is given.

So, let us seek the LORD because He alone is worthy of all pursuit. Let us seek to know Him personally and intimately through His word—the Bible. Let us seek to grow in the faith He has given us, so we will know Christ and His Heavenly Father with an ever increasing joy! Yes, we have needs—*especially during this time*—but let those be secondary reasons for us drawing near to Jesus. May we draw near to our Lord and Savior just because we love to be in His Presence. After all, when two people are in love—"just because" is enough.

He is worthy of all praise, glory and honor!

"Whoever believes in Me, as Scripture has said, rivers of living water will flow from within them." - John 7:38 (NIV)

What flows from within you? How do other people experience your life? Do they retreat when they see you coming? Are people drained after talking with you? Or are they built up and encouraged by your words and actions? Jesus states that His followers will have "rivers of living water" flowing out from within them. This is not dramatic, poetic, flowery language. Jesus is not using some kind of metaphor, but rather is revealing what happens when His spiritual supremacy meets our personal reality.

To the one who believes in Him, as Scripture has declared, rivers of living water will flow from their inner-most being. Do you realize what He is saying? There is a realm of existence which only comes about for those who *believe* in Him. There is a level of living which can only be accessed and experienced by those who *trust* in Him. So, to the level that we believe, that is the level of life-giving water we will experience. For all of us who say, "well this is just the way I am. I can't change," Jesus says, "No. We can be different!" He can say that because He's the One who makes us different. Do you believe His words?

Let's take a closer look at what He says by reading it in the Amplified Bible: *"He who believes in Me **[who adheres to, trusts in, and relies on Me]**, as the Scripture has said, 'From his innermost being will flow continually rivers of living water.'"*

Our belief *begins* with agreeing that God exists. Then it grows into knowing that Jesus is the Son of God and us committing our lives to Him. Then it becomes the expectation of Christ's promise—the indwelling of the Holy Spirit *(vs. 39)*. Then we learn how to trust in and rely on Christ in every situation. That leads us to become increasingly obedient to Him—which gives the Holy Spirit more room to operate within us. As He does, we are transformed from glory to glory *(2 Corinthians 3:18)*. In the process, Jesus our Savior becomes Christ our Lord and the person we once were—apart from Christ—is replaced by God's new creation *(2 Corinthians 5:17)*!

The transformative power of God's living water begins as a stream and grows to a raging river of life! Jesus says that those who adhere to Him, trust in Him, and rely on Him, will experience what is otherwise *impossible*—a life-giving, regenerative, restorative flow. Remember when Jesus spoke to the Samaritan woman at the well *(John 4)*? He told her that if she drank the living water He gave, then she would never thirst again. It wasn't physical thirst He was referring to, but rather the spiritual drought within her soul which separated her from God and caused her to make bad decisions.

We need to realize that this continual flowing doesn't come *from* us. The Holy Spirit is both its Source and its Substance! And the rivers of living water isn't only for us either. *As God flows in us* and the overflow builds, *God will flow through us* and use us to be a blessing to others. This Christian life truly is not one where we are alone trying to do things on our own. **God's Holy Spirit flows through each of His children—using us for His glory—while preparing us to be with Him for all eternity.** What God is doing is both marvelous and mysterious in our eyes. Praise be to Jesus Christ!

PRAYER: Heavenly Father, thank You for Your precious Holy Spirit. Please help me to give You ever-increasing room within my heart, mind and body. May You get the full glory and honor out of my life! In Jesus' Name. Amen.

ACTION: Write the Scripture verse from John 7:38 in bold letters on a sheet of paper. Make copies and place it in multiple places to remind you of its truth. If you're really daring... put some water in a sealed clear bag labeled "Living Water" and carry it around during your day as a constant reminder of God's Holy Spirit dwelling in you.

DAY 23

DON'T TAKE IT PERSONAL
May 6, 2020

I don't know if you have seen the movie, The Matrix. It's a science fiction film which shines a light on systems of control. In the movie, human governmental systems exist, but there is a "system behind the system," where artificial intelligence machines use an advanced digital reality simulation to enslave the human race. Lawerence Fishburne plays the character, Morpheus, whose primary job is to help open people's eyes to the truth and free them from the tyranny of the machines.

When Morpheus meets Neo (Keanu Reeves), he helps free him from "The Matrix." He then teaches him how the Matrix works to enslave people. He explains that those who are plugged into the world system are unknowingly being influenced by the "machine system." And they will fight to protect the system from those who try to free them from it.

Why am I bringing this up? In today's devotional you will discover that the Bible tells us about a "system within a system." A system not ruled by machines, but by Satan. And those who are still plugged into the fallen system will fight against we who have been freed—even though we seek to help them.

In Christ, you are free! Jesus is worthy of all praise, glory and honor!

18 "If the world hates you, keep in mind that it hated me first. 19 If you belonged to the world, it would love you as its own. As it is, you do not belong to the world, but I have chosen you out of the world. That is why the world hates you. 20 Remember what I told you: 'A servant is not greater than his master.' If they persecuted me, they will persecute you also. If they obeyed my teaching, they will obey yours also. 21 They will treat you this way because of my name, for they do not know the one who sent me." -John 15:18-21 (NIV)

Parents usually teach children to be likable so people in the world will accept them. On the surface, this is good. We *should* know how to be friendly and able to work with others. **But here, Jesus is telling us there is a deeper spiritual dynamic which makes likability with the world impossible: there will be moments when the world hates us—all because we belong to Him.** This is a hard truth for many, because the love of the world is tempting. We seek to find purpose in the world. We want to find belonging in the world. For example, just look at what happens when the Gospel is combined with the American dream. What we get is not the true Gospel of Jesus at all.

When Jesus talks about the world, He means *the fallen systems of governing which exists at every level of social interaction.* That includes the internal motivations of self and others who are plugged into the world system. This "world system" promotes and glorifies everything that stands in opposition to God. The Bible makes it clear that while God owns all creation, the fallen world system is run by Satan, who is the "god of this world" and the "prince and power of the air." Satan also blinds the eyes, hearts and minds of unbelievers and works overtime to keep them from coming to the knowledge of the truth which is found in Christ Jesus. *(2 Corinthians 4:4; Ephesians 2:2)*

By telling us ahead of time that the world will hate us, because it has hated Him, Jesus is saying, ***"Don't take it personal."*** While the attacks may be directed at you and me, realize that people are attacking us because—as the saying goes—*their arms are too short to box with God.* While we feel like it's a "personal" attack on us, it is really the dark ruler of this fallen world system lashing out in fear at God's image bearers.

The devil realizes that we have what he can never get: redemption and forgiveness of sins. And that maddens him. His destiny is sealed. He rebelled against God with his eyes wide open. He deceived a third of the angels to rebel with him, with his eyes wide open. He knew exactly what he was trying to do when he declared he wanted to take God's place as ruler over all creation. Humanity on the other hand, rebelled out of a manipulated ignorance. And while our rebellion puts us in line for the same judgment which awaits the devil, God loved us so much that He sent Christ to make a way of escape for us.

So, Jesus tells us that ***we are no longer of the world***. Because of this, we should no longer live as if the world is the "only show in town." We are now to live to please Christ and our Heavenly Father. And if persecution comes because we love Jesus, then let it come. When it does—and we stand firm in our faith toward Him—then great is our reward in heaven! *(Matthew 5:10-12)*

Romans 12:1-2 encourages us to present our bodies as living sacrifices to our Lord. We are to allow God's Word to transform our minds so we can know and be obedient to God's will and purpose. <u>We are told to go through the process of *unlearning* all of those things that makes us view reality from the</u>

perspective of the fallen world system. This falls in line with what Christ tells us in today's devotional Scripture. Instead of seeking to please the world and make our kingdoms *in it*, we are to please God and look forward to that "building not made with hands" (2 Corinthians 5:1).

This doesn't mean God won't bless us in the "here and now." He does, so we can point others to Him. *What it means is that we are not to live as if this world system is our home—because it is not.* We have become citizens of heaven *(Philippians 3:20-21)*! Life eternal awaits every believer in Christ Jesus! The more we internalize this truth that Jesus shares, the more we will be ready to stand firm when persecution comes.

PRAYER: Heavenly Father, thank you for giving me life in this world. Even more so, thank you for granting me eternal life in the world to come! Help me prepare for my true home in Your kingdom. And help me not to take things personal when someone comes against me just because I love You. In Jesus' Name. Amen.

ACTION: Study what the Bible says about the nature of the "spiritual matrix" which Satan uses to keep people blinded from God's truth. Make a plan to share what you learn with those you care about. Then do it.

DAY 24

CITIZENS OF HEAVEN

May 7, 2020

When my wife gave birth to our son, he became part of our family. He also, at that moment, became a citizen of the United States of America. As a 9 year old, he rarely focuses on being a citizen. He just likes being a child in the family. But, as he grows to understand how the world works, so he will begin to understand what it means to be a citizen of this country. And the more capable he becomes in life, the more he will need to understand the rights, privileges and protections granted to the citizens of this country.

This is true of us as Believers in Christ. We are children of the King and citizens of a Kingdom. But we often talk of being God's child and rarely mention being a citizen of heaven. Is our focus so much on this world that we can't see the value of our spiritual citizenship? May today's devotional draw our attention higher, so we can see—while we are citizens of earth, even more importantly, through Christ we are citizens of heaven! And our heavenly citizenship is good for all eternity!

Jesus is worthy of all praise, glory and honor!

14 "Do not let your hearts be troubled. You believe in God; believe also in me. 2 My Father's house has many rooms; if that were not so, would I have told you that I am going there to prepare a place for you? 3 And if I go and prepare a place for you, I will come back and take you to be with me that you also may be where I am." -John 14:1-3 (NIV)

When we are born again, God makes us His children through the power of His Holy Spirit *(John 3:3-8)*. We are adopted into God's family *(Ephesians 1:5)*. Jesus also makes us *citizens* in His kingdom *(Philippians 3:20)*! We often think of ourselves as *children of God*, but perhaps not as *citizens of God's Kingdom*. However, even in the natural we see an example of this spiritual truth at work: *at the moment of our birth as children, we also become citizens of the "place" where we are born.*

Jesus left earth to prepare a place for us in His Father's Kingdom and He will one day return to take us there. This means we have dual citizenship. We are born on earth, but now belong to heaven! Being *"children"* speaks to the intimacy we can have with our Heavenly Father, through Christ. Being a *"citizen"* speaks to something else: *our duty and responsibilities.* A citizen is: *a native or naturalized member of a town, city, state or nation who owes allegiance to its government and is entitled to its privileges and protections.*

So, what does being a citizen of heaven look like? Here are 7 central aspects:

1. Citizens of heaven serve Christ and others out of love *(Matthew 22:36-40; John 14:15)*.

2. Citizens of heaven have roles in God's Kingdom *(Luke 22:29-30)*. Here, Jesus tells His disciples they would be granted the privilege to rule in His kingdom—one such role is to judge the 12 tribes of Israel. This lets us know that *we too* will have roles to play.

3. Citizens of heaven are to be ambassadors for Christ *(2 Corinthians 5:11-21)*. An ambassador is: *a diplomatic official sent by one country to represent its interests in a foreign land.* As ambassadors for Jesus, *in this world,* our duty is to

represent the interests of our Lord, by living out the truth of His Gospel. *(Matthew 28:18-20; John 20:21; Colossians 1:12-14)*

4. Citizens of heaven are *no longer of this world (John 15:19; 17:16-19)*. Christ has chosen us out of the world. Because our *heavenly citizenship* is to become our ***primary identity***, we will encounter opposition from those who are still a part of this world's fallen system.

5. Citizens of heaven have access to the privileges, rights, provision and protection of God's Kingdom. *This means we can "call heaven down" on our earthly situations. (Matthew 6:9-13; 7:7; 16:19 / Luke 11:1-4 / John 14:10-14 / 2 Corinthians 10:3-5 / Ephesians 6:10-18 / Philippians 4:4-7, 19 / Hebrews 1:14 / 1 John 4:4)*

6. Citizens of heaven are spiritually seated with Christ, even though we are physically on earth *(Colossians 3:1-4)*. We are encouraged to focus our hearts and minds on "heavenly kingdom matters," instead of being consumed with earthly temporal gains. When Christ returns, our earthly location and heavenly position will be united together.

7. Citizens of heaven are made to be priests in God's kingdom —in order to serve Him now, in heaven in the future and reigning with Him on the new earth *(1 Peter 2:9-10; Revelation 5:10-11)*. This sounds like God's original intent that humanity would have rulership over the earth *(Genesis 1:26-28)*. It also speaks to the future, where Jesus Christ returns to vanquish evil and makes all things new. We will then reign with Him forever (Daniel 7: 13-14,18, 21-27; Revelation 20-22).

It is impossible to exhaust, in one devotional, what our heavenly citizenship means. But in the coming days, months and years—as Christian persecution increases—knowing who you are as a child of God and as a citizen of heaven will be extremely important to accept, understand and live by. May we take time to know the One who is both the Way to the Father and the King of kings. Amen.

PRAYER: Heavenly Father, thank you for making me a citizen of heaven through Your Son, Jesus. Please help me to live now in light of then. In Your Son's Name I pray, Amen.

ACTION: This is a project you can do by yourself or with others. Create your own Citizen of Heaven Passport! (Use a real passport as a template for your design starting point.) Include the list from today's devotional within its pages. Also include other key Scriptures which speak to your identity in Christ. Carry this with you during your daily travels and read it often as a reminder of your heavenly citizenship.

DAY 25

WHOSE GLORY ARE YOU SEEKING?

May 8, 2020

Jesus makes it very clear what it means to be His disciple. The Jesus we see who loves and blesses children with a smile, is the same Jesus who commands our total allegiance. When Jesus says, "Follow Me," He isn't giving a suggestion. He is making a declaration. And when we actually follow Him, we are declaring our dependence on Him. In today's devotional, we will read some teachings of Jesus which will challenge us.

Remember when God challenges us with truth, it isn't to push us away. It is to help us see through the lies which keep us bound, so we can be free. Free to be everything God has called us to be! Free to know Him and worship Him in spirit and in truth! Free to participate with God in His plan of salvation so others can be set free! So, read with expectation! Be honest with God and yourself about where you currently are in your relationship with Him. Then ask Him to help you close the gap so you can walk with Christ with ever increasing joy and faith!

Jesus is worthy of all praise, glory and honor!

"How can you believe since you accept glory from one another but do not seek the glory that comes from the only God?" - John 5:44

The motivation behind what we do matters. Two people can complete the same exact "good work," but one is received by God and the other is not. Why? Because one sought personal glory and the other sought glory for God. Things always go bad when someone seeks the wrong glory. Egos get enlarged. Pride enters the heart. A fall of some sort is waiting in the wind (Proverbs 16:18).

Jesus says in Matthew 6:1, *"Be careful not to practice your righteousness in front of others to be seen by them. If you do, you will have no reward from your Father in heaven."* He goes on to give examples of what this looks like: making a big deal when giving to the needy *so others will honor us*. Praying on street corners *so others can see us and think we are so spiritual.* Praying long prayers *to try and impress others and God with our vocabulary.* We can probably find other examples, but you get the picture.

Jesus indicates, in both Matthew 6 and John 5, that accepting glory from others in order to make a name for ourselves *always* gets in the way of our relationship with God. Jesus asks in today's Scripture, **"How can you believe since you accept glory from one another but do not seek the glory that comes from the only God?"** What does He mean? Accepting glory from others—AKA—being overly concerned with what others think about us—*can actually KEEP US from believing in who Jesus is!*

Let that sink in for a moment... **If we are overly concerned with what others think about us... and we are overly concerned with our own view of ourselves... these conflicts will keep us from believing in who Jesus is.** As we journey through life, we will have *many opportunities* to choose between accepting glory from others or seeking the glory that only God can give. What matters most to us? Our own opinions? The opinion and approval of others? Or God's opinion and approval of us? Which of these will be central in powering our motivations in life? Understand that each leads to a different destination. As we try to answer this question for ourselves, here are several teachings of Jesus for us to consider. They are challenging, but they are true.

"Then He said to them all: 'Whoever wants to be My disciple must deny themselves and take up their cross daily and follow me." - Luke 9:23

32 "Whoever acknowledges Me before others, I will also acknowledge before My Father in heaven. 33 But whoever disowns Me before others, I will disown before My Father in heaven." - Matthew 10:32-33

37 "Anyone who loves their father or mother more than Me is not worthy of Me; anyone who loves their son or daughter more than Me is not worthy of Me. 38 Whoever finds their life will lose it, and whoever loses their life for My sake will find it." -Matthew 10:37-39

26 "If anyone comes to Me and does not hate father and mother, wife and children, brothers and sisters—yes, even their own life—such a person cannot be My disciple. 27 And whoever does not carry their cross and follow Me cannot be My disciple." -Luke 14:26-27

PRAYER: Heavenly Father, help me to not take the glory which belongs to You alone. In Jesus' Name. Amen.

ACTION: When someone congratulates you on a job well done… Say thank you and then give the glory to God.

DAY 26

THE CENTRAL WORK OF GOD
May 9, 2020

We often wonder what God wants from us. We often ask what can we do for Him? We often question where God wants us to be, where we are to go, how we are to live? We say, "I wish I knew what I was supposed to do!"

In today's devotional, we will see that people came to Jesus with the same kind of questions. What was His response? A straightforward—yet multi-layered—answer. May we take His answer to heart and put it into practice. Everything we could possibly do in life depends on it. And that is no exaggeration!

Jesus is worthy of all praise, glory and honor!

28 "Then they asked Him, "What must we do to do the works God requires?" 29 Jesus answered, "The work of God is this: to believe in the one He has sent." -John 6:28-29 (NIV)

This is one of my favorite Scriptures in the entire Bible. I'm not sure why I love it so much. I just know I do. Here, people come to Jesus with a sentimentality most of us have towards God today. *"What can I do for you, Lord?"* *"How can I work FOR God?"* *"Will you please bless MY plan to bring you glory?"*

Let's be clear—*God doesn't NEED our help with anything*. He is perfectly capable of accomplishing everything He desires on His own. Having said that, Scripture reveals that even though

God *can* do all things on His own, He often *desires* to use the works of His hands (humanity and the created order) to accomplish His plans. So, He *DESIRES* to use us. His desire is a *privilege He shares* with us. And that privilege should not be taken for granted.

While we desire to work FOR God, _God desires to work IN us!_ And this is at the heart of Jesus' reply to the inquiry in John 6. **We often want to do things for God without having to change who we are.** We want to work within our own skillset, mindset and heart-set. We want to work within our own power and according to our own knowledge. But Christ comes to us directly with the truth. In essence He says: *"God's idea of work that pleases Him is very different from your idea of work."* Here are His actual words from the New International Version of the Bible: **"The work of God is this: to BELIEVE in the one He has sent."**

In other words, *Christ lets us in on the secret of secrets...* **_the battle in life is for our belief in who HE IS!_** Every situation and circumstance revolves around our perception of the identity of Jesus Christ. I say "perception" because **Jesus knows who He is**—it is we who have a difficult time seeing Him clearly. He says this is where we should be working—in growing and maintaining our belief in Him. *Because only here will eternal life be manifested in us. Only here will we discover who Christ is, who we are in relation to Him, what He's called and created us to do and how we are to carry out what He's planned for us (Ephesians 2:10).* We chase after these things apart from Him. We try to create our own meaning, our own standards and our own purpose. _Yet, Christ lets us know that everything we are looking for, what we truly need is summed up and found **IN HIM.**_

This is why the devil fights us so hard in the area of belief. This is why we struggle so much with fear, doubt and unbelief. This is why Satan works so hard to keep us from reading, studying and understanding the Bible. This is why the fallen world system—which he controls—works overtime for our attention and seeks to subvert, twist and pervert God's true message. Satan does not want us to see Jesus for WHO HE TRULY IS! If we did, then everything would change! And so he seeks to blind us (2 Corinthians 4:3-4).

This is why you and I can be wide awake when watching television and suddenly fall asleep when we try to read the Bible and pray. There are forces fighting against us. But, if we begin to *believe correctly* about who Jesus IS then everything in our life will begin to change! Jesus Himself said in Mark 9:23, ***"Everything is possible for one who believes."*** *Here, He means for the one who believes rightly about who HE IS and places their trust and reliance in Him.*

Jesus knows having a right belief about who He is, translates into us being in a loving and obedient relationship with Him. Our love and obedience then translate into God having full access to us through His Holy Spirit. The greater God's access to our heart, mind, body and resources, the more impactful our lives will become because we will be working in concert with Christ Himself! We have been so busy trying to DO things without Him and Jesus has been saying all along, ***learn how to BE with Him.***

You and I can build monuments to Christ, feed the homeless in His name and do a host of other things. But if we never truly submit our hearts and minds to His Lordship then everything we do will be in vain (Matthew 7:21-23). Plenty of people do "good" things in God's name—without ever surrendering their lives to Christ—thinking that their deeds are enough to get them into God's good graces. If they do not repent, what shock they will find on Judgment Day to stand before God's throne and discover that it was **always** about having a right belief in Jesus.

"This is the work of God, that you believe in the one He has sent." Do you believe in Jesus? Just what do you believe about Him? Was He just a man? Do you believe He was merely a good teacher or prophet? Or is He Christ—the Messiah—the Son of the Living God? The Son of Man. Your King. Your Lord. Your Master. Your Savior.

PRAYER: Heavenly Father, help me to focus on the central work of Your heart… to truly believe in Your Son Whom You have sent. In His Name I pray. Amen.

ACTION: ONE: List the things of the world that you love the most: favorite entertainment, foods, etc. TWO: Set a reasonable timeframe to step back from those things so you can focus more on knowing Christ through His Word, prayer and worship. THREE: Incorporate into your daily routine periodic times of "stepping back from the enticements of the world," so you can feed your spirit and grow in Jesus.

DAY 27

WHAT GIVES YOU LIFE?

May 10, 2020

Where do you go to find life? When you are down, confused, tired, angry, how do you find your way back to a place of wholeness? Some people eat, watch their favorite shows, others listen to music, go out into nature, etc… But after we do these things, if God is not at the center, we find there is still an emptiness. That emptiness is the result of the fundamental way God has made us. He has created humanity to be in communion with Him. And though some things can make us feel good for a time, without Christ, we can never find complete and total fulfillment.

So, when we find ourselves in these situations, let us remember to go to the Source of True Life—Jesus Himself— and allow Him to work within us. Let's ask Him to lead and guide us. *Jesus came so we might have life and have it more abundantly! And that life is found in Him through His Word.*

Jesus is worthy of all praise, glory and honor!

"The Spirit gives life; the flesh counts for nothing. The words I have spoken to you—they are full of the Spirit and life." - John 6:63 (NIV)

Think about what Jesus says… *The Holy Spirit gives life. His words are full of the Spirit and life.* There is a power exchange which happens in the spirit realm that has a tremendous effect

91

on us in the physical! How does He heal, deliver and set people free? With a word. How does He defend against the attacks of Satan? With a word. How does He raise someone from the dead? With a word. In these situations the "flesh counts for nothing." The flesh hasn't the power to bring deliverance on its own. Why? Because of its sinful condition. It is only when Christ speaks what He has heard His Heavenly Father speak that situations change. It is only when He does what He sees His Heavenly Father do that change happens. *(John 5:19-20)*

In this singular statement, Jesus lets us know that the Holy Spirit is to take precedence over our flesh. He says this to a people who live in a world system where the flesh is elevated to the supreme pursuit. Flesh is pampered and indulged. Practically everyone works to satisfy their desires and needs. Hedonism reigns. Yet, Jesus says humanity's way of living is backwards, misguided and inside out. We seek life in pursuits that can never truly satisfy. The hunger of our fleshly nature can never be satisfied by our fleshly nature. This reminds me of the Albert Einstein quote:

"We can't solve problems by using the same kind of thinking we used when we created them."

We have a sin problem and think that indulging in more sin or personal self-help techniques will correct it. But Jesus says that our fleshly nature ultimately does not profit us. Do we truly believe that it is Christ's Spirit which gives us life? Do we believe that when it comes to eternal matters (which is essentially all matters) our flesh is sorely inadequate to get the job done? *Do we believe that in everything we do and are, we are supposed to be drawing our strength and sustenance from Christ himself?*

What did Jesus say when He was tempted by the devil to turn the stone into bread? *"Man shall not live by bread alone, but by every word that proceeds from the mouth of God" (Matthew 4:4).* Again, He states the order of priority. The Spirit must come first if we are to truly experience life as it was meant to be known. Are you living by bread alone (flesh) or are you living by every word which comes from the mouth of God?

Jesus declaration runs against the grain. It is counter-cultural and counter intuitive. It can make us uncomfortable. It seems unreachable… impossible even. And even if we try to make the switch, our flesh will rebel! That's because it's used to getting its way.

We don't even know how to fully live in reliance on the Spirit. **But doesn't it sound inviting?** If we belong to Christ, somewhere within us our spirit cries out "Yes!" And Jesus tells how those of us who desire to know Him can grow in the Spirit… **by His words.** *The words He speaks to us are full of the Spirit and life!* How much of Christ's words do we read and listen to on a daily basis? How vital are His words to us above the words of anyone else we encounter in life? How important are His words to us at any given point of the day? *The more time we spend with Him, through His words, the more transformation and power we will inevitably experience!*

PRAYER: Heavenly Father, thank you for Your Son Jesus. Please help me to listen to His words more and more so I can truly live like You desire me to live. In His Name I pray, Amen.

ACTION: Begin to read and/or listen to chapters of the Gospel of John each day. List/mark the teachings of Jesus which stand out to you. When you finish go to Matthew, then Mark and then Luke. Once complete—repeat.

DAY 28

THE NECESSITY OF HIS SCARS — PART 1
May 11, 2020

Have you ever wondered why, when you heal from an injury, a scar remains? Every now and then the question crosses my mind. Also, did you know there are some species of life on earth that can heal from injury without *any scarring* at all? Wouldn't it be amazing if we could do the same—leaving no evidence that there was a prior problem?

But, when I look at my scars, they give me a snapshot of a moment in time. They tell a story. The scar on my left temple is from 4th grade—we don't have space here for *that* story. The scar on my left hand came from a glass shattering while I was washing it. The scar on my right forearm came from accidentally brushing up against a hot iron. Even while reading these words you may be thinking about your own scars...

We all have scars and those scars tell a story. Today, our devotional looks at a moment in time when Jesus' disciples needed to see His scars and be reminded of the Story that matters most. May we be reminded as well.

Jesus is worthy of all praise, glory and honor!

"Then He said to Thomas, "Put your fingers here, see my hands. Reach out your hand and put it into My side. Stop doubting and believe." -John 20:27 (NIV)

Thomas refused to believe what the others told him. The night of that first Sunday was glorious! It was true: Jesus was alive! He had visited His disciples while they were behind locked doors. One minute He wasn't there and the next moment… He was! They thought He was a ghost! But Jesus identified Himself and allowed them to touch His body—especially His scars. Luke 24:41-43 tells us that He even ate with them! They believed! But there was a problem. For some reason, Thomas was not present.

After Jesus vanished from their sight, the disciples were overjoyed and didn't know what to do with themselves. Then Thomas knocked on the door, and they let him in. Can you picture it? He was probably wondering why they were all smiling from ear to ear. Their eyes wide with excitement as if their entire bodies were about to burst. They were like children desperately trying to hold onto the biggest secret ever! I imagine Thomas looked warily at them all as they rushed him inside while closing and locking the door up tight.

"What's wrong with you guys? Why are you all smiling?"

"We have seen the Lord," they exclaimed—probably in unison… and with jumping… and with glee… and singing!

But Thomas doesn't react in the same way. Before they could get into the details, he cuts them off cold: *"Unless I see the nail marks in His hands and put my finger where the nails were, and put my hand into His side, I will not believe."* (vs. 25) Thomas is in a hard place. He's heard all day from several different people that Jesus was seen alive. Now, his comrades in ministry tell him the same thing with complete assurance and confidence, yet Thomas refuses the truth. No doubt, they told him what happened when Jesus came to them. On the surface, Thomas craved the same experience with Jesus that they had. But on a deeper level, he was resolute in his unbelief.

A week later, all of the disciples—including Thomas—are locked in the house again. Jesus appeared suddenly—startling them. Everyone's momentary fear turns to joy as Thomas' eyes go wide in awe and his mouth drops open. Jesus calms the group and then immediately addresses Thomas' unbelief.

"Put your fingers here, see My hands. Reach out your hand and put it into My side. Stop doubting and believe." (vs. 27)

Thomas's hands tremble as he examines Jesus' scars and (most likely) falls to his knees while exclaiming, *"My Lord and my God!"* (vs. 28)

Then Jesus told him, *"Because you have seen me, you have believed. Blessed are those who have not seen and yet have believed."* (vs.29)

Jesus endured great physical punishment and mutilation leading up to His crucifixion. He was scourged with a whip that contained sharp metal bits. A crown of thorns was pressed into His skull. He had bruises from falling on the road while carrying the heavy crossbeam up to Golgotha. He was nailed to the cross, hoisted high for everyone to see, and thrust through with a spear. His appearance at the point of death made Him almost unrecognizable! *But, at His resurrection, all of His injuries were healed without a trace—***except for the nail marks and the spear incision.** *Have you ever wondered why Jesus still has these scars?* We will look deeper at this question in the next installment.

PRAYER: Heavenly Father, please help me to understand the necessity of Christ's scars. In Jesus' Name, Amen.

ACTION: Do a study on Jesus' crucifixion and resurrection. Begin with the accounts in the gospels. Then read/watch "The Case for Christ" by Lee Strobel. Also, read/watch talks on the resurrection by Dr. Gary Habermas.

DAY 29

THE NECESSITY OF HIS SCARS — PART 2

May 12, 2020

In the last devotional, I asked if you have ever wondered why —after His resurrection—Jesus still has the scars from His crucifixion? Today's devotional seeks to answer this question. Whether you have contemplated Jesus' scars or not, it is worth us considering now. It is my prayer that Christ moves on your heart so you can know Him better.

Jesus is worthy of all praise, glory and honor!

"Then He said to Thomas, "Put your fingers here, see My hands. Reach out your hand and put it into My side. Stop doubting and believe." -John 20:27 (NIV)

Evidence. Jesus provided His disciples with irrefutable evidence to prove they were not hallucinating. He was, in fact, standing before them—fully resurrected—and not as some kind of phantom. To prove His argument, He presented "Exhibit A" detailing His scars and the Story they conveyed. Why the scars? Because they show, without a shadow of a doubt that it was Jesus—in the SAME BODY—the disciples saw up on the cross and then placed in the tomb. The scars are the proof that they were talking with the One and Only Jesus! And for the next 40 days, Scripture tells that Jesus provided many more convincing proofs to His followers of His resurrection and the reality of God's coming kingdom. *(John 21:25; Acts 1:3)*

The scars are proof of God's plan of salvation. Jesus' crucifixion fulfilled the *prophecy of Isaiah 53*—which was written approximately 680 years before Jesus scaled Calvary's hill. That central Jewish prophecy *spans the entire chapter* and heralds the coming of the Messiah to willingly sacrifice His life to save humanity from their sins by satisfying God's wrath on sin. Here are three verses from the chapter.

4 "Surely he took up our pain and bore our suffering, yet we considered him punished by God, stricken by him, and afflicted. 5 But he was pierced for our transgressions, he was crushed for our iniquities; the punishment that brought us peace was on him, and by his wounds we are healed. 6 We all, like sheep, have gone astray, each of us has turned to our own way; and the LORD has laid on him the iniquity of us all." - Isaiah 53:4-6 (NIV)

The scars are necessary because they prove Jesus' love for His Father. *Philippians 2:6-11* reveals He was obedient to His Father, even to the point of death. His obedience resulted in His unrivaled exaltation that all creation will acknowledge. His scars also prove His love for humanity. He came to seek and save the lost *(Luke 19:10)* and completed every step in the plan of salvation in order to rescue us! *(John 19:30)*

As His body healed during the act of resurrection, **Jesus made a conscious decision to keep these scars**. They proclaim His lasting victory over sin and death, for He will never die again *(Revelation 1:17-18)*! He became the Firstborn among many brothers and sisters—for He will raise us to life with powerful bodies like His on the last day; *and we too, will never die again (John 6:40; Romans 8:29; Philippians 3:20-21)*! His triumph proves that even in humiliation, "our God reigns!" *(Colossians 2:13-15; Hebrews 12:1-3)*

His scars are necessary because God's redemption Story began before time itself. Before the foundation of the world, God had already decided to step into His own creation. He would become human in order to free us from the true villain of our souls: the devil *(1 Corinthians 2:6-8; 1 John 3:8; 1 Peter 1:20)*. God declared peace with us, through the blood Jesus shed on the cross *(Colossians 1:20)*. Through His blood, we are made part of a brand new humanity! *(Revelation 5:9-10)* Sin, death and Satan are now on borrowed time. The day of their destruction is fast approaching! *(Daniel 7; Revelation 20)*

There is no greater Story than what Jesus Christ has accomplished! He inaugurated His Kingdom on the cross and displayed its power at the tomb. By the Holy Spirit, He bestows His Kingdom into the heart of everyone who places their faith in Him. This makes us citizens of that Kingdom! He departed to heaven to prepare a place for us in His Kingdom *(John 14:1-4)*. One day, He will return with the angels and saints to establish His Kingdom here on earth! Then everyone will know that Jesus of Nazareth is LORD, to the glory of God the Father *(Philippians 2:10-11)*! At that point, Jesus will vanquish evil and make all things right in the world. Then we will truly understand the price He paid to redeem us.

Every interaction with Christ in the New Heaven and on the New Earth will be a reminder we will never forget. Not in a, *"I told you so"* manner, but with a, *"I love you so"* boldness! Every glance at our Savior's hands and feet—every hug brushing up against His side—will proclaim the abundant love of God! The scars He has chosen to keep are the evidence! And throughout the annals of eternity—as we enter what is humanly impossible to comprehend and imagine—the Story of Christ's redemption will ring true in the universe and beyond *(1 Corinthians 2:9-10)! And Christ will continue to serve as the*

Foundation—the Eternal Chief Cornerstone—upon which all other glories are built.

PRAYER: Heavenly Father, thank you for saving me through Your Son's sacrifice. Please help me to live in a way that honors Christ's scars. In Jesus' Name, Amen.

ACTION: Share your study on Jesus' crucifixion and resurrection with others.

DAY 30

COME!

May 13, 2020

We all have issues with trusting God. In some areas, we and God are good! In other areas... not so much. We pray and He speaks... and we find excuses not to obey. This happens when we allow the facts of the situation to steal our focus away from Christ. If we can keep our eyes trained on Jesus, we will discover that He will often provide us with a specific word and plan of attack in order to successfully navigate through life's storms. As He brings us through every situation, we must remind ourselves that Jesus is building purpose and strength in us so we can bring Him glory.

Jesus is truly worthy of all praise, glory and honor!

27 "But Jesus immediately said to them: 'Take courage! It is I. Don't be afraid.' 28 'Lord, if it's you,' Peter replied, 'tell me to come to you on the water.' 29 'Come,' he said. Then Peter got down out of the boat, walked on the water and came toward Jesus." - Matthew 14:27-29 (NIV)

We don't know how Jesus walked on water. As Creator and Sustainer of the universe, He clearly had mastery over the very atoms of matter and the physical forces which govern their movement through time and space. But, as God in the flesh, Jesus was not limited to the usage of mere physics. My speculation is that He could have reduced the effect of the gravitational field around Him, making Him light enough to walk on water. (After all, water does have surface tension which allows small insects to walk on it). Or He could have increased the surface tension of the water beneath His feet— making it solid enough to support His weight. Maybe there's a third option yet to be considered! However Jesus did it, the sight of Him walking the waves must have been amazing!

Yet, that was not the *only* miracle Jesus performed. Peter had enough *faith-filled-nerve* to make a bold request. Sure, he was scared, but he knew within Himself, if it truly *was* Jesus, everything would be alright. And if Jesus displayed **this kind of power**, it would be nothing for Him to add "one more person" outside the boat. So, with a single word Jesus **enabled** Peter to walk on water! Whatever power Jesus used to defy the pull of gravity immediately went to work for His disciple as well! Peter became the second person in all of human history to walk on water! And then... he took his eyes off of Jesus and focused on the impossibility of the moment... and sank like a stone!

But let's not focus on the sinking. Peter proved that the impossible was possible. *Rather, Jesus proved that the impossible was possible for Peter.* Some of us like to say, *"well Jesus **was Jesus**. That's why He could do the impossible. I'm just little old me."* In a sense that is correct. The Power Source for Peter's gravity defying feat did not come from him. So, under any other condition, Peter would have been completely and utterly incapable of walking on water! However, what made the impossible possible was two-fold: **Peter's faith placed in Jesus AND Jesus' affirmative response.**

"Lord, if it's you," Peter replied, *"tell me to come to you on the water."*

"Come," He said. Then Peter got down out of the boat, walked on the water and came toward Jesus.

It's all about coming to Jesus. Peter's faith was tied into Jesus' identity, His ability and His willingness. Because Jesus *was really Jesus*, He had the ability to make Peter a co-participant in the impossible. As the Son of God, Jesus also had the authority to call Peter out onto the deep waters. Even though Peter wasn't perfect, His desire had always been to be as close to Jesus as possible. This situation proved to be no different. Jesus was willing to honor Peter's request and allowed Him to do what He Himself was doing. Notice too, that Jesus was the one doing the "heavy lifting." *Peter's part to play was to believe, keep His eyes on Jesus and keep walking towards Him.*

What can we learn from Peter's walk with Jesus on the waves? When we pray to God about a situation and He responds in the affirmative—**revealing His Will**—we can go ahead and step out of the boat—even if the rest of our group decides to play it safe! *(Note: Don't step out if God isn't telling you to do so.)* God wants us to be obedient to His calling and commands for our lives. This happens as we grow in our belief, trust and reliance on Christ through His Word. This is our part. *Jesus always provides His power when we/His people have the ability to take Him at His word.*

PRAYER: Heavenly Father, thank you for giving us these examples in Your Word. Help me to be like Peter—to be able to call out to Jesus in times of trouble and to be obedient to His command. In Jesus' Name, Amen.

ACTION: Spend time reading the account of Peter walking on the water. What other insight can you find?

DAY 31

WHOSE WILL ARE YOU FOLLOWING?

May 14, 2020

I've watched my son's personality develop for the last 9 years. What an amazing and humbling experience! Some of his character traits are "mirror images" of me when I was his age! In other ways he acts just like his mother. Yet, he has certain personality traits which seem to be all his own. As my wife and I watch him grow, we often pray about who he is becoming and ask for the Lord's guidance during this season. While we have our own expectations, we realize God has His own set of expectations for our son.

Having to raise a child has been one of the ways God has opened up the Scriptures to us. Teaching our son about love and obedience has made us more sensitive to living a life that is pleasing to the Lord. May today's devotional help you see that with God as your Heavenly Father, the one expectation that truly matters most of all is His.

Jesus is worthy of all praise, glory and honor!

"For I have come down from heaven not to do my will but to do the will of Him who sent Me." -John 6:38

We each have a will. From our will flows the desire to pursue and achieve goals in life. Our wills are determined by the interactions between our internal thoughts, impulses and the outside world—what we like and don't like, what we fear, what we are attracted to, what brings pleasure and what repulses us, etc. Additionally, our wills are also shaped by our response to the expectations of the people in our lives: our parents, extended family, neighbors, friends, enemies, teachers, mentors, employers, religious leaders, politicians, entertainers, and so on. But what about God? Do we seek to know His will for our lives so He can shape us?

One of the worst things that can happen is to get to the end of our life and discover we've spent all of our time going in the wrong direction. We've pursued a purpose God did not want us to pursue. What a tragedy! This begs the question: Who is the most important person in our life?

The Bible invites us to follow Jesus as our example. After all, Jesus did say to each of His disciples, **"Follow Me."** So, what do we see when we look at His life on earth? It was a *hierarchical balance* between following His Heavenly Father and meeting the expectations of others—*when they were in line with His Father's will*. For example, at twelve years old, His parents lost Him for three days after the Passover festival. When they found Him in the Temple He said, *"Why were you searching for me? Didn't you know I had to be in My Father's house?" (Luke 2:49)*

His Father was first. However, the balance is seen in Luke 2: 51-52: "Then he *[Jesus]* went down to Nazareth with them *[His parents]* and was obedient to them... And Jesus grew in wisdom and stature, and in favor with God and man."

As a man, during His three-and-a-half years of ministry, Jesus declared the following:

"...Very truly I tell you, the Son can do nothing by himself; he can do only what he sees his Father doing, because whatever the Father does the Son also does." (John 5:19)

"My food," said Jesus, "is to do the will of Him who sent Me and to finish His work." (John 4:34)

"...Father, I thank you that you have heard me. 42 I knew that you always hear me, but I said this for the benefit of the people standing here, that they may believe that you sent me." (John 11:41-42)

"Father, if you are willing, take this cup from Me; yet not my will, but yours be done." (Luke 24: 42)

Jesus' words from our devotional Scripture sums it up well: ***"For I have come down from heaven not to do my will but to do the will of Him who sent Me."***

I know His words might rub us the wrong way. After all, we have our own wills, dreams, goals and aspirations! We have been told that we should "follow our heart." "We can be whatever we want to be and do whatever we want to do!" "We can discover what we're passionate about and pursue that!" And at the opposite end of the spectrum, we may have encountered some very controlling people who have tried to coerce and manipulate us in directions that weren't good for us. Because of this, we are very protective of our own desires. Yet, where does God fit into all of this?

Jesus comes by each of us and says, ***"Follow Me."*** Then He reveals that in order for us to be His disciples we must love Him more than anything and anyone else—including our desires *(Matthew 10:37-39; 16:24-25; Mark 8:34-35; Luke 9:23-24)*. Jesus also tells us there are two paths we can follow—one leads to eternal life and the other leads to eternal destruction *(Matthew 7:13-14)*. So, what will we do? Will we trust God's will, dreams, plans and purposes for our lives? Or will we reject His will in favor of pursuing our own goals?

The prospect of surrendering our will to God can be terrifying. But if we do, God will *redirect* some desires and completely *replace* others—all for His glory and our good *(Romans 8:28)*. **Ephesians 2:10** has brought me great comfort in this area: *"For we are God's handiwork, created in Christ Jesus to do good works, which God prepared in advance for us to do."* ***Knowing God has determined what He wants me to do has freed me from the pressure of figuring things out on my own.*** As I seek to know and love Jesus, He provides what I need to fulfill His purpose for my life. *(Matthew 6:33)*

As we learn to trust Christ, we will discover the plans our Heavenly Father has reserved for us *are the best plans for us*. Then we can say like Jesus, "I live to do the will of my Father in heaven." Whatever the earthly outcome may be, it will be well worth hearing these words as we enter eternity: *"Well done, good and faithful servant! You have been faithful with a few things; I will put you in charge of many things. Come and share your master's happiness!" (Matthew 25:21)*

PRAYER: Heavenly Father, help me to see that You have the best plans for me. Please give me the desire to submit my desires to You so I can follow You. In Jesus' Name, Amen.

ACTION: Make a list of all of your plans. Then present them to God in submission and ask Him to give you clarity on His will for your life. Ask Him if you should pursue your plans. If so, then how should you pursue them? If not, then what should you be pursuing? Based on what God reveals, be ready to restructure or replace the plans you have listed.

DAY 32

A WONDERFUL TRUTH

May 15, 2020

I want you to "hear" me... **_God is able to take care of you._** Your heavenly Father is fully capable of leading you, providing for you and protecting you. You belong to Jesus, so His Holy Spirit indwells you and makes you a part of His family. It is by His Spirit that God will bring you through any situation you face, so you can know Him more intimately and bring Him increasing glory. It is also by His Spirit that God moves on the hearts and minds of your sisters and brothers in Christ to provide help in troubling times.

Today's devotional Scripture will present a wonderful truth Jesus shares with us. Then I will share life experiences where I've seen this truth in action. With everything going on in the world, we need to be reminded that God is intricately involved with each one of us... because we belong to Him. And if He is with us, then we can follow Him from now into eternity.

Jesus is worthy of all praise, glory and honor!

29 "Are not two sparrows sold for a penny? Yet not one of them will fall to the ground outside your Father's care. 30 And even the very hairs of your head are all numbered. 31 So don't be afraid; you are worth more than many sparrows. - Matthew 10:29-31 (NIV)

How many times have you thought about sparrows? Most of us—never. Do you know how many strands of hair you have on your head—*If you're not bald?* Here, Jesus uses an illustration of two seemingly insignificant things to reveal *a wonderful truth* that we sometimes find hard to believe: **God cares about the intimate details of our life.** He shares this illustration to help us understand that God truly does take care of us.

Have there been times when it seemed farfetched that God cared about "everything" you cared about? Why can we believe Jesus *for salvation*, but have a hard time trusting Him for our daily needs? "Sparrows and numbered hair" were foreign concepts to me until God spoke in a language I could understand. Allow me to share four instances:

ONE: I grew up on comic book superheroes! But as my faith in Christ grew, I wanted to see heroes who *believed* like me. One day, in 2002 while creating my own character, I thought about two famous superheroes who wield hammers. I prayed: *"Lord, Ephesians 6 talks about the Sword of the Spirit, but too bad there isn't a biblical basis for my character to have a hammer."* Two weeks later at church, my pastor was teaching and said, *"You know the Bible says that God's Word is like a hammer."* I was shocked! Sure enough, Jeremiah 23:29 reads, *"Is not my word like fire,"* declares the LORD, *"and like a hammer that breaks a rock in pieces?"* Does God care about comic book superheroes? I don't know... but it sure became apparent God cared about me in that moment.

TWO: Around 2005, I was in a canoe on a river in West Africa. While filming hippopotamuses in the water with my video camera, a dragonfly landed right next to me. Just so you know, dragonflies are my absolute favorite insects in all the world! So, I started filming it—and an interesting thing happened: *the* *dragonfly fluttered its wings, but did not fly away!* It stayed still the entire time I videoed it. And once I was fully satisfied with my video coverage, *then* it flew away! Our heavenly Father cares about the sparrows... Apparently, He cares about dragonflies too... and a young black man from New York who was half-way around the world in West Africa!

THREE: One day, I watched a documentary on rocket belts— that people strap to their backs so they can fly. A Texas-based company made them. A few years later, in 2008, I was in Texas for a conference and emailed the company to see if they gave tours. They invited me to stop by. The owner gave me a great tour, let me strap into the rocket belt *(No, I didn't fly it), and* took me to lunch. We both discovered we were Christians! Then he said to me, *"We usually don't give tours. When your request came in, I was going to tell you, 'NO'. But, during my morning devotional time, **God told me to let you come.**"* I was speechless and humbled! Apparently God cares about rocket belts... or at least about the two guys—one black and one white—who were interested in them.

FOUR: One day I lost track of time at work and had to pick my son up from school and take him to swimming class. While driving, I asked God a "top level" question: *"LORD, what do You want me to do with my life? What ultimate purpose will define my next 5-10 years?"* God's two-word answer was clear as day: ***"SWIMMING BAG!"*** YIKES! I had forgotten my son's swim bag at home! This would make me *even later*, but he had to go to swim class. I made a u-turn and laughed while thanking Jesus for His practicality! I was thinking about "eternal" matters. He was instructing me on an immediate issue which would affect my son's ability to swim and my wife's reaction—*if he had missed his class because of me!* God saved me on *multiple* levels that day!

If you stop and think about it, you have times like these—where Christ meets you in the "small moments." When Jesus says His Father cares about the "sparrows and your hair," you should take Him at His word. God is not just interested in our crisis moments where big decisions have to be made. He's also concerned about the small moments we think are too insignificant and trivial for the One who rules the entire universe. That's part of the beauty of the Resurrection Life Christ came to give us! Our Heavenly Father takes into account every aspect of who we are and who we are becoming in Christ. This is just one astounding reason why He's worthy to be praised at all times!

Don't forget: *God is intricately involved with you... because you belong to Him. So don't be afraid; you are worth more than many sparrows.*

PRAYER: Heavenly Father, You are worthy to be praised at all times. Thank you for letting me know that You care about every aspect of who I am. After all, You are the One who created me. Please help me to be all that You desire me to be. In Jesus' Name I pray, Amen.

ACTION: Take some time to look back over your life for "sparrows and hair" situations. Write down those times when God provided for small desires or situations you encountered.

DAY 33

ALMOST ISN'T ENOUGH

May 16, 2020

There's a Flonase television commercial that showcases a dog "almost" fully shaved, a table "almost" fully dusted and a lawn "almost" fully cut. The voiceover says: "You wouldn't accept an incomplete job from anyone else…" We understand in these types of situations that "almost isn't enough." I wonder what God thinks about this as it relates to us?

Yes, we aren't perfect. We are not capable—on this side of eternity—of sinless perfection. Yet, Christ *does* call us to follow Him. As we will see in today's devotional, a central aspect of following Christ is being obedient when He points out those things we need to give up and leave behind. Why does He do this? Because He loves us and wants us to follow Him fully—mistakes and all. <u>Jesus is not looking for sinless perfection; but **He is** looking for us to *remain with Him* so we can be perfected by Him!</u>

Jesus is worthy of all praise, glory and honor!

"Jesus looked at them and said, 'With man this is impossible, but not with God; all things are possible with God." - Mark 10:27 (NIV)

Jesus had just finished a conversation with a rich young ruler. This guy had everything he could ever want, except a true and abiding relationship with God. He had the religious etiquette and formalities. He knew the commandments. He even had the *intention* of following God—up until a certain point. He probably looked for Jesus to give him a pat on the back while saying, *"You're doing great!"* Instead, Jesus looked at the man with love and compassion and told him the "whole truth and nothing but the truth."

"This one thing you lack. Go sell everything you have and give to the poor, and you will have treasure in heaven. Then come follow Me." Jesus verbally pressed His finger on the pulse of the young man. He exposed the fact that the man ultimately found his identity in his wealth. It would be impossible for him to be everything God wanted him to be until he was willing to let it all go and focus on following Christ. The young man couldn't take it and walked away sad because he had many possessions. This makes me wonder: do we find our ultimate identity in Christ?

Notice that Jesus doesn't chase him down to tell him to come back. He watches him go. Then He turns to His disciples and says, *"It is easier for a camel to go through the eye of a needle than for a rich person to enter the kingdom of God."* His disciples are astonished, because having wealth was seen as a sign of God's blessing. *"Well then, who can be saved?"* they ask. He responds, *"With man this is impossible, but not with God; all things are possible with God."*

We often quote this verse when we are trying to forge ahead through difficulty and obstacles in order to reach our goals. However, the context of this Scripture isn't about that at all. Rather, it's about our total inability to reach God based on our own merits. Jesus is saying, *"Almost isn't enough, but God is able to do the impossible! He can reach down and save sinners."* It is also here that Jesus reveals a necessary ingredient for salvation: humility.

Contrary to popular belief, when Jesus mentions the "eye of a needle" He is not talking about a *sewing needle*. Rather, the term refers to a low, narrow gate or passageway. When a person traveled, the camel was the equivalent of the "family car." It carried the person and the luggage. When traveling through mountainous desert locations, the traveler would oftentimes encounter a small, narrow passageway in the wall of a city or between rocks. In order to get through, the person would get off the camel and offload the luggage. The camel would have to get down on its knees and shuffle its way through the passageway. Once on the other side, it could stand up again, the luggage could be placed on it and the voyage could continue.

So, when Jesus says, *"it's easier for a camel to go through the eye of a needle than for a rich person to enter the kingdom of heaven,"* He is saying that wealthy people have difficulty humbling themselves. Why? Because they can buy whatever they want, live wherever they want, dress however they want and treat others however they want. But, wealth, social status and a resume of philanthropic advancements can't get anyone into heaven. In order to get into the kingdom of God, a person must humble themselves before Christ.

We may or may not be wealthy like the rich young ruler, but we may have the same issue of pride—thinking we can "work our way into heaven." *The transformation God wants to do within us is impossible... **without Him.*** The reality God is calling us to is impossible to achieve on our own. Salvation is impossible without surrendering our hearts to Jesus. And this surrendering must lead to a willingness to follow Christ—daily—and rid ourselves of whatever He says is holding us back from Him. *(Luke 9:23)*

PRAYER: Heavenly Father, I am incapable of making myself presentable to You on my own. There are moments when I make mistakes. And there are moments when I rebel against Your commands. Please forgive me. I humble myself before You and ask that You help me to remain with You so You can continue Your work of perfecting me for Your kingdom. In Jesus' Name I pray, Amen.

ACTION: Take some time to seek Jesus through prayer and His Word. Inquire about what He may be asking you to give up so you can follow Him more truly. Ask for His strength to leave behind whatever He reveals. Then do it and don't look back.

DAY 34

DEATH LEADS TO LIFE!

May 17, 2020

I am no gardener. But I do understand when you plant a seed, the protective shell that is needed above ground—to keep the seed safe before planting—must be broken below ground once it's planted. This happens so the roots can grow and the plant can sprout up. After a while, the size of the plant is many times bigger than the seed that once contained it.

Today's devotional Scripture speaks to this phenomenon and relates it to eternal life. May we realize that whatever Christ requires us to sacrifice now in order to serve Him, He will make sure we yield a great crop of Resurrection Life—in this world and in the world to come!

Jesus is worthy of all praise, glory and honor!

24 "Very truly I tell you, unless a kernel of wheat falls to the ground and dies, it remains only a single seed. But if it dies, it produces many seeds. 25 Anyone who loves their life will lose it, while anyone who hates their life in this world will keep it for eternal life. 26 Whoever serves me must follow me; and where I am, my servant also will be. My Father will honor the one who serves me." - John 12:24-26 (NIV)

Jesus is referring to the fact that He has to die in order to usher God's Resurrection Life into the world. It is only in His death—as the Ultimate Seed—the Seed of the woman as prophesied in Genesis 3:15—does the way become possible for those of us who believe in Christ to become God's offspring. Romans 8:29 puts it this way: *"For those God foreknew He also predestined to be conformed to the image of His Son, that He might be the firstborn among many brothers and sisters."*

Then, Jesus makes the connection between what He is about to do and what He calls us to do. In order for the Resurrection Life to work fully in us, we must be willing to relinquish whatever God tells us to let go from this world. This is the only way for us to pursue the "higher" life He died and rose to give us. This is how the Amplified Bible puts it:

24 *"I assure you and most solemnly say to you, unless a grain of wheat falls into the earth and dies, it remains alone [just one grain, never more]. But if it dies, it produces much grain and yields a harvest. **25** The one who loves his life [eventually] loses it [through death], but the one who hates his life in this world [and is concerned with pleasing God] will keep it for life eternal. **26** If anyone serves Me, he must [continue to faithfully] follow Me [without hesitation, holding steadfastly to Me, conforming to My example in living and, if need be, suffering or perhaps dying because of faith in Me]; and wherever I am [in heaven's glory], there will My servant be also. If anyone serves Me, the Father will honor him."*

Do you see it? Jesus comes right out and encourages us to give up any worldly pursuit in favor of pursuing Him. Anything that we love more than Christ will eventually be on God's chopping block. He tells us that the person who wants eternal life has to cease from living this life under their own estimations. **Rather, they must allow God *to be* their estimation.** If they can do that, then He will reveal what He wants them to pursue and how to pursue it.

Are we willing to die to ourselves? Are we willing to sacrifice our plans and agendas—our hopes and dreams which live apart from Christ? When we live for ourselves, we seek to live for our own glory. But when we submit our will to Christ and learn how to let Him lead our pursuits, then we live in service to Him—which is to live for God's glory. The life that is lived in service to Jesus is the life that will spend an eternity in the direct Presence of His glory. And Jesus declares that His Father will honor the one who serves the Son. Wow! I wonder what that honor will look like?

PRAYER: Heavenly Father, You are worthy of being praised at all times. Please help me to serve Your Son. May I live this life for Your glory and look forward to receiving honor from You in the world to come. In Jesus' Name I pray, Amen.

ACTION: Take an honest look at those things you love more than Christ. Present them before God and ask Him to help you put them in their proper place… subservient to Him.

DAY 35

THE TEACHER'S EXAMPLE

May 18, 2020

We often second-guess God's Word because we don't see how it can possibly apply to the situations we are facing. We may think that Scripture written more than two thousand years ago doesn't take into account our modern-day sensibilities and concerns. However, second guessing the Scriptures has nothing to do with the timeframe we live in.

In today's devotional, we see that Peter second guessed Jesus. In fact, when we read through the Bible, we see people —in every generation—who thought that God's Word did not apply to them. May we see that God's Word is applicable to every generation and situation, because it is authored by The One who created all things and who rules time and space.

Jesus is worthy of all praise, glory and honor!

"No," said Peter, "you shall never wash my feet." Jesus answered, "Unless I wash you, you have no part with me." - John 13:8 (NIV)

So many of us want to be self-sufficient. We have our pride, our dignity and can do things on our own. There are certain actions that we deem to be beneath us. Peter was like this too. He watches as his Master disrobes himself, wraps a towel around his waist, takes a basin full of water and begins to wash His disciples' feet. It makes no sense to Peter's sensibilities nor to our own. Why would the Master, whom the disciples serve, turn and serve the disciples in a way that seems beneath Him? Jesus knows they don't yet understand what He is doing *(vs. 7)*. Peter's reaction proves the point. As soon as Jesus comes to him, he declares, *"You shall never wash my feet."*

Have you ever been to a foot washing? I have been to several. They all start out the same way... with reluctance. We don't want to expose our feet to be washed because we are ashamed of their condition. And many, myself included, didn't necessarily *want* to wash someone else's feet. But, Jesus **did** leave us this specific example, didn't He? But an interesting thing happened at these foot washings. The hesitancy disappeared as we all participated together. Humility replaced shame as feet were washed while prayers were uttered. Foot washing is an intimate act. Both the washer and the one whose feet are being washed must humble themselves before God and each other.

So, Jesus makes a truth statement that is so blatantly confrontational it can seem harsh. *"Unless I wash you, you have no part with Me."* He is very clear here... In essence He says, **"there is no self-sufficiency in the kingdom of God— only God sufficiency."** All must rely on Christ to be cleansed, redeemed, reconciled and received into the grace of our Heavenly Father. There is no other way. THERE. IS. NO. OTHER. WAY.

When Peter was confronted with the gravity of the situation, he pleaded with Jesus *(vs. 9)*: *"Then, Lord, not just my feet but my hands and my head as well!"* Ah, that Peter... always so bold in his exclamations! Jesus lets him know only his feet need to be washed. For the feet are what come into the most contact with the world. Each day our feet encounter the dirt, filth and stresses of life. Sometimes our feet lead us to places we shouldn't go. During Jesus' day, people wore sandals, so the feet were exposed to even more elements. This is why a person's feet would be washed before they entered into someone's home. A person may not have realized just how dirty his or her feet were, until they were exposed and washed.

Jesus ends the entire lesson for His disciples by saying in verses 13-17, *13 "You call me Teacher and Lord, and rightly so, for that is what I am. 14 Now that I, your Lord and Teacher, have washed your feet, you also should wash one another's feet. 15 I have set you an example that you should do as I have done for you. 16 Very truly I tell you, no servant is greater than his master, nor is a messenger greater than the one who sent him. 17 Now that you know these things, you will be blessed if you do them."*

This new humanity God is creating... this resurrection community... is to be made up of people who live humbly before God and each other.

PRAYER: Heavenly Father, help me not to live by my own sufficiency, but rather by Yours. Please, wash my feet and help me to wash the feet of others. In Jesus' Name, Amen.

ACTION: Plan and participate in a foot washing. Not just with people you like, but also with those you may not be fond of being around. Use this devotional's Scripture passage as the foundation. Have a time of prayer while each person takes turns washing and being washed.

DAY 36

THE BRIDEGROOM IS COMING!
May 19, 2020

It's amazing how we can read the same Scripture multiple times and see the same thing. Then one day, we read it and God opens our eyes to see something that was always there—yet hidden from our view! That "something new" isn't actually a thing at all—but a Person: JESUS. May today's devotional help you see Christ more clearly.

Jesus is worthy of all praise, glory and honor!

"At that time the kingdom of heaven will be like ten virgins who took their lamps and went out to meet the bridegroom." - Matthew 25:1

Many of us are familiar with this parable—at least on the surface. Jesus tells of five wise virgins and five who are foolish. They all had lamps with oil to keep the flames burning, but only five thought ahead and brought extra oil in case it took longer than expected for the bridegroom to arrive. *The bridegroom did take longer than expected*—in fact verse 5 tells us that he took so long in coming that the ten virgins became drowsy and fell asleep!

I stated that most of us only have a surface relationship with this parable because we often read it in isolation—separate from the context of the chapters around it. If we looked at this parable in context, we would immediately notice that it is a part of Jesus' larger teaching on His Second Coming. At the beginning of chapter 24 verse 3, Jesus' disciples ask, *"When will the temple be destroyed and what will be the sign of your coming and of the end of the age?"* The "end of the age" means that point in time when Jesus breaks in on human history to settle all accounts, vanquish evil and reign on the earth. Jesus takes two chapters—24 and 25—a total of 94 VERSES—to answer their two-part question! From verses 4-31, in chapter 24, Jesus gives a timeline of major events which must take place before He returns. In verses 32-51, He tells His followers (us included) to remain watchful. Jesus then uses verses 1-30 of chapter 25 to give two parables which illustrate His teaching. Then He closes out the chapter (verses 31-46) with a description of all humanity standing before Him on Judgment Day—the day the Son of Man returns in His glory with the angels with Him.

When we read the parable of the ten virgins, we often give our attention to the differences between them. But there is one glaring similarity: they ALL fall asleep! The ten virgins represent the Church. Whether wise or foolish, they **all** allowed the excitement of the coming wedding feast to wear off. We often focus on the virgins as "them," but in reality... they are "us." We are all in various stages of sleep... Jesus has taken an awfully long time to come for us, so we have lost the excitement and joy that are associated with His return. When a person sleeps, he or she is oblivious to their surroundings and often dream of things that don't truly exist and can never satisfy. Similarly, we have spent our lives being asleep— oblivious to the reality of Christ which surrounds us. We spend all of our energy "dreaming" of and working on ways to create our own kingdoms here on earth. The Real Thing is replaced by substitutes, which will never satisfy us.

The shame is not in us falling asleep. After all, Jesus said, "the spirit is willing, but the flesh is weak" *(Matthew 26:41)*. But it is shameful if when God shakes us with His message, we *remain* sleep. Jesus told His disciples then and is telling us now: it is time to wake up so we can be prepared for His coming! His call to His Church is that we live in such a way as to daily prepare for God's Kingdom to arrive—because He is coming again! It's time to "wake up" and shake off our drowsiness! It's time to trim our lamps and make sure we have enough oil (Holy Spirit) while there is still time! Midnight is approaching when the cry will ring out: *"Here's the bridegroom! Come out to meet Him!" (vs. 6)* Don't you want to be ready?

Finally, while we spend so much time focusing on the ten virgins, the main character of the parable is actually the **BRIDEGROOM**. Do you know who He is? Everything centers around Him and His big day *(Luke 24:25-27)*. The parable also infers that the five wise virgins were so enamored with the bridegroom that they made the necessary preparations to ensure they were ready to meet Him when He finally arrived. Are you doing the same while there is still time? He wants you to be ready. The **BRIDEGROOM** is coming and His name is **JESUS**! Only those who wake up and are ready will be received by Him when He parts the sky.

PRAYER: Heavenly Father, please help me to wake up and regain the excitement for the coming of the Bridegroom—Your Son! May my lamp be filled with oil and may my excitement be contagious so others will awake as well and be ready. In Jesus' Name I pray, Amen.

ACTION: In what ways do you need to wake up?

DAY 37

THE SON OF MAN!

May 20, 2020

Do you know which term Jesus used to refer to Himself the most in the Gospels? Was it Christ—the Messiah? What about Son of David? Or Son of Man? Or was it Son of God? You may be wondering, *why does it even matter?* Well, would you agree that Jesus is always very deliberate about what He says and does? He never minimizes or exaggerates the truth—because HE IS TRUTH! (John 14:6)

In today's devotional, we will look at the title Jesus used the most to refer to Himself. We will also seek to uncover why it matters? What we will discover has the potential to change our view of Jesus forever!

Jesus is truly worthy of all praise, glory and honor!

63 "But Jesus remained silent. The high priest said to him, 'I charge you under oath by the living God: Tell us if you are the Messiah, the Son of God.' 64 'You have said so,' Jesus replied. 'But I say to all of you: From now on you will see the Son of Man sitting at the right hand of the Mighty One and coming on the clouds of heaven.' 65 Then the high priest tore his clothes and said, 'He has spoken blasphemy! Why do we need any more witnesses? Look, now you have heard the blasphemy." - Matthew 26:63-65 (NIV)

Why does it seem that Jesus is so tight lipped about His true identity? Why doesn't He just come right out and say, "I'm the Messiah, the Son of God?" Yes, He does tell specific people who He is—like His disciples and the woman at the well. But Jesus isn't as quiet about it as we might think. We just need to understand the terminology He uses—one in particular—and its meaning. That term is: *Son of Man*. Many people believe that the term only refers to Jesus being fully human. After all, this term is used in the Old Testament—such as Ezekiel—to speak of regular human beings. However, in Daniel 7 the term has a much greater—exalted—meaning!

Think about it... the term must have meant something **MONUMENTAL** if when Jesus declared it before the religious council at His trial, they all tore their clothes in response. It must have been **EARTH SHATTERING** because they screamed He had committed blasphemy—making Himself equal with God! In fact, when giving His answer as to whether He was the Messiah and the Son of God, Jesus' use of *Son of Man* was a direct reference to Daniel 7:13-14. It was *this reference* that caused His opponents to cry out. Let's take a look at it—the vision Daniel was given of the Last Day:

13 "In my vision at night I looked, and there before me was One like a Son of Man, coming with the clouds of heaven. He approached the Ancient of Days and was led into His presence. 14 He was given authority, glory and sovereign power; all nations and peoples of every language worshiped Him. His dominion is an everlasting dominion that will not pass away, and His kingdom is one that will never be destroyed."

The *Son of Man* in Daniel 7, is clearly *MORE THAN HUMAN.* This Person, who approaches the Ancient of Days (God the Father) is: ONE: Led into God's Direct Presence. (God told

Moses no mere man can see His face and live). TWO: This Person is given ALL authority, glory and sovereign power. THREE: This Person is worshiped by all people on earth. FOUR: This Person has dominion and a kingdom that is everlasting and will **never** be destroyed. The Son of Man in this passage is none other than God the Son receiving His kingdom at the End of the Age! *(Isaiah 2:1-5; Hosea 6:1-3; Joel 3; Zechariah 14; Philippians 2:9-11; 1 Corinthians 15:20-28; Revelation 1:1,7,12-18; 19:11-21; 20:1-15; 21:1-8)*

So, when Jesus used this term during the trial before His crucifixion, His opponents knew **EXACTLY** what He was saying: He is the Messiah they were waiting for. He is the Son of God. But the religious leaders were blinded by their own biases and expectations that the Messiah would come to free Israel from Roman oppression. **Yet, Jesus came to first free the human heart from sinful oppression.** *(Read Isaiah 53).* After all, what good is it to be physically free, if we are still bound by sin, spiritually, mentally, emotionally and relationally?

Daniel 7 sounds a lot like Jesus' declaration about Himself when He returns at the End of the Age:

30 "Then will appear the sign of the Son of Man in heaven. And then all the peoples of the earth will mourn when they see the Son of Man coming on the clouds of heaven, with power and great glory. 31 And He will send His angels with a loud trumpet call, and they will gather His elect from the four winds, from one end of the heavens to the other." -Matthew 24:30-31

31 "When the Son of Man comes in His glory, and all the angels with Him, He will sit on His glorious throne. 32 All the nations will be gathered before Him, and He will separate the people one from another as a shepherd separates the sheep from the goats." -Matthew 25:31-32

Son of Man was the preferred title Jesus used for Himself in the Gospels. He referred to Himself by this term **78 times**! This was way more than when He referred to Himself as "Christ"—the Messiah, the "Son of God" and the "Son of David." By referring to Himself as the *Son of Man,* Jesus unequivocally connects Himself to Daniel's vision of the Only One who can free humanity by defeating evil once and for all! Therefore, shouldn't we pay close attention to how Jesus self-reveals to us? The Day of His Return is fast approaching and we need to be ready!

PRAYER: Heavenly Father, please give me increasing understanding of how Jesus is the Son of Man. In Jesus' Name I pray, Amen.

ACTION: Bible Study! Read Daniel 7. Then read through the four gospels (Matthew, Mark, Luke and John) and highlight each place where Jesus refers to Himself as the Son of Man. Look at each of those instances through the lens of Daniel 7. What is Jesus saying?

— — —

NOTE: For a deeper study on Jesus as the Son of Man, read the following two books from One King Publishing by author Samuel Whitefield.

Son of Man: The Gospel of Daniel 7 (Vol.1)
Son of Man: The Apostles' Gospel (Vol. 2)

DAY 38

THE CHURCH THAT CHRIST BUILDS
May 21, 2020

Did you know that there are churches which don't belong to Christ? They are "churches" in name only, but the people don't follow Jesus. I remember the story of a well-to-do congregation looking for a pastor. The candidate came and was told by the pulpit committee, "You can't preach about Jesus, sin, nor hell here. But you can talk about the nice parts of the Bible and about current events." This begs the question: Is a church a "church" if Jesus isn't invited into their midst? Jesus Himself said, "Where two or three gather in My name I am there with them." (Matthew 18:20) So, the answer to the question would be, "No."

In today's devotional we look at Christ's ownership of the church. The fact that we belong to Him should influence what we do in this life. After all, Christ is coming back for a Bride (the church) that is radiant, without blemish, holy and blameless. *(Ephesians 5:25-27)*

Truly, Jesus is worthy of all praise, glory and honor!

17 "Jesus replied, 'Blessed are you, Simon son of Jonah, for this was not revealed to you by flesh and blood, but by My Father in heaven. 18 And I tell you that you are Peter, and on this rock I will build My church, and the gates of Hades will not overcome it." - Matthew 16:17-18

Jesus asked His disciples who the crowds said that He—*the Son of Man*—was. The overall consensus was that He was a prophet. Then Jesus asked His disciples, *"But who do you say that I am?"* Peter replied, *"You are the Christ, the Son of the living God."* Jesus commended Peter for listening to the voice of His Heavenly Father. Then He affirmed Peter's name and identity. In the Greek, *"Peter"* is **Petros** and means, *a small rock or detached stone.*

Jesus then declares, *"and on this rock I will build My church; and the gates of Hades will not overcome it."* The Greek word here for *"rock"* is **Petra**, which means, *bedrock or a huge rock.* Notice the wordplay Jesus uses. He is not proclaiming Peter to be the first Pope of the church, but rather Christ is declaring that Peter's identity is found in Christ, as he participates in the work Christ is doing. What work? Jesus is building His Church! And just as Jesus took fishermen to fish *for* people, Jesus is the Carpenter who builds a building made *with people. (1 Corinthians 3:9; 2 Corinthians 5:1; Ephesians 2: 19-22; 1 Peter 2:4-7)*

Scripture is clear: Jesus is clearly depicted as both the foundation and the Chief Cornerstone of the church. *(1 Corinthians 3:13; Ephesians 2:19-22).* Since Jesus is the foundation upon which the church stands, then we can only find our true identity as we follow Christ. The clearer we can see who Christ is, the clearer we see who we are in relation to Him and each other. The clearer our vision, the better we can work for the purposes of God's Kingdom, instead of being distracted by the lures of the world.

Church—in the Greek—is **Ecclesia**. It means, *an assembly. The whole body of the redeemed, all those whom the Father has given to Christ, the invisible universal church.* When Christ-followers assemble together in particular places, they are considered local congregations. The wonderful thing about

Christ's church is that it is not limited to merely the buildings in which we gather. We can lose the building or be restricted from meeting in person and still be the church! Church *happens* whenever two, three or more persons gather together in the Name of Jesus *(Matthew 18:20)*. "In His Name" means that we gather to be about His Business. <u>His Business is, *to seek and to save the "lost" AND to grow and mature the "found" so we can bare fruit for the glory of God the Father.*</u> It is a sad day when the church has lost sight of her LORD and becomes busy doing work that is more aligned with the ways of the fallen world system rather than the ways of Christ.

Jesus is in the process of finishing up His work building His church. One day soon, He will be done. On that day, He will return. In the meantime, the gates of hell have done everything possible to try and destroy Christ's church. In every generation since Christ established His church, Satan has inspired the jailing and killing of Christians, the burning of Bibles and the demolishing of local congregational buildings. He has also inspired the changing of laws to silence the message Christ gave the church to share with the world. Satan has sought to bribe the church, to coerce the church, to manipulate and deceive the church. The devil has fought to scare the church, to blind and smother the church and to invade the church. Whatever the gates of hell have thrown at the church, may have won some battles, but never the war!

Christ's declaration that "the gates of hell shall not overcome His church" still proves to be true! His true and genuine church will stand the test of time because she belongs to Christ alone! *It is for Him that we live, for Him that we breathe, for Him that we work and for Him that we die.* And it is because of Him that Resurrection Life will course through our veins on the Last Day —and we will rise fully restored with power! *(John 6:38-40)*

When Jesus returns—parting the sky in all of His glory—His church will then be fully conformed into His image and made perfect *(Romans 8:29; Ephesians 5:25-27)*! Christ seeks to liberate humanity and creation from the gates of hell *(Romans 8:16-23)*! He has created His church—*those called out of the world and into relationship with Him*—to be co-laborers in His work of salvation and discipleship making! We are the ambassadors of Christ called to tell a dying world that they can receive the Living Savior—while there's still time.
—*(2 Corinthians 5:20-21)*

Are you a part of the church that Christ is building?

PRAYER: Heavenly Father, thank you for making me a part of Your Church through Your Son. Please help me to be a witness unto Christ to a world that desperately needs Him. Help me to stand firm with other sisters and brothers in Christ, even when the gates of hell uses multiple means to try and cause us to retreat from Your call. May I remember that the true church belongs to Jesus! And He will soon be done with His building. Hallelujah! In Jesus' Name, Amen.

ACTION: Take a serious look at your life. In what ways are you living for Jesus? In what ways are you not? How can you bridge the difference?

DAY 39

KING OF KINGS AND LORD OF LORDS
May 22, 2020

May Jesus Christ—*the Son of Man*—*Our Bridegroom*—*the King of Kings and Lord of Lords*—be praised and worshiped to the glory of God the Father! And may we eagerly await His return! The Day draws near!

Jesus is worthy of all praise, glory and honor!

31 "When the Son of Man comes in His glory, and all the angels with Him, He will sit on His glorious throne. 32 All the nations will be gathered before Him, and He will separate the people one from another as a shepherd separates the sheep from the goats. 33 He will put the sheep on His right and the goats on His left. 34 Then the King will say to those on His right, 'Come, you who are blessed by My Father, take your inheritance, the kingdom prepared for you since the creation of the world. 35 For I was hungry and you gave Me something to eat. I was thirsty and you gave Me something to drink. I was a stranger and you invited Me in. 36 I needed clothes and you clothed Me. I was sick and you looked after Me, I was in prison and you came to visit Me. 37 Then the righteous will answer Him, 'Lord, when did we see You hungry and feed You, or thirsty and give You something to drink? 38 When did we see You a stranger and invite You in, or needing clothes and clothe You. 39 When did we see You sick or in prison and go to visit You? 40 The King will reply, 'Truly I tell you, whatever you did for the least of these brothers and sisters of mine, you did for Me. 41 Then He will say to those on His left, 'Depart from Me, you who are cursed, into the eternal fire prepared for the devil and his angels... 45 He will reply, 'Truly I tell you, whatever you did not do for one of the least of these, you did not do for Me. 46 Then they will go away to eternal punishment, but the righteous to eternal life." -Matthew 25:31-41, 45-46 (NIV)

It's amazing that the wind and the waves, the periodic table elements, gravity, plants and animals, cells in our bodies and even demons obey the commands of Jesus. Yet, humanity's fallen sin nature resists God at every turn. But, to those who respond when Jesus knocks on the door of their hearts—who willingly submit themselves to Christ and finish the race He has laid up for them—*an eternal inheritance awaits*—all to the infinite joy and glory of Christ and His Father!

What a Day that will be... when the veil of reality is finally pulled back completely and everything is seen for what it truly is. Those on "top" will be on the bottom. And those at the "bottom" will be placed on top. Those who enjoyed the pleasures of this life without caring about knowing Christ and serving His Kingdom, will have all eternity to contemplate their failure in the eternal fire prepared for the devil and his angels. And those who gave up whatever Jesus commanded in order to follow Him more closely, more perfectly and more intimately —those who suffered in numerous ways for the Name and Character of Christ—will have all eternity to contemplate the grace and love of God, as they carry out new responsibilities for His glory, devoid of any hint of boredom, dissatisfaction or sinful weakness.

The existence that awaits the Christ-follower is so unimaginably astounding that the devil works this present darkness overtime—the fallen world system—to keep us distracted and alienated from God's Truth. But on the Last Day, when Christ returns on the clouds of heaven in all of His majestic glory and with His powerful angels by His side, the question of **Who is truly in charge** will be answered in full *(Revelation 19:11-16)*! Every eye will see Him! Every knee will bow! Every tongue will confess that Jesus is LORD to the glory of our Heavenly Father! *(Philippians 2:10-11)* Yes... **our Heavenly FATHER.** Jesus makes it clear that He and His Father are transforming us from servants, to friends to siblings of Christ—making us God's children! *(Matthew 12:48-50; John 15:15; John 20: 17; Romans 8:16-39))*

And so, we will see in full... that this entire journey of sheep following their Good Shepherd was entirely worth it! Jesus Christ will reign on earth from the throne of David in Jerusalem! We will celebrate Him as life will be restored beyond overflowing! Weakness will give way to strength. Sickness will be washed away by health. Death will be destroyed. Evil will finally be vanquished and all things that please God will be celebrated! You... will be celebrated by the One who sees all of the sacrifices you make for His glory *(Zephaniah 3:9-20)*! Then our SAVIOR, our LORD AND KING, our BRIDEGROOM, the SON OF MAN will create a New Universe! The old will pass away and we will reign with Him forever!

So, from now until That Day when Christ parts the sky, may we who love Him be His witnesses *(Acts 1:8; 2 Corinthians 5:20)*! And may we shout from the top of our lungs: *Maranatha! Which means,* **"Come, Lord Jesus, Come!"**

PRAYER: Heavenly Father, help me to see Your Son Jesus fully as my King. Please give me the grace to remain faithful to You through the end. For You declare that those who endure to the end will be saved. In Jesus' Name, Amen.

ACTION: Make a poster of Jesus' titles. Place it where you can see it to remind you of the One you are ultimately living for.

DAY 40

THY KINGDOM COME!
June 1, 2020

This is the 40th Day of us seeking to understand more about Christ's Resurrection Life. At the beginning of this journey, I highlighted how Jesus spent 40 days, after His resurrection, teaching His followers more about God's Kingdom. My desire was to help us do something similar by deliberately spending 40 days looking at the words of Jesus. This attempt to write these devotionals has been limited by my own human failings. I have never had to write consistently for 40 days straight! However, I could feel the Holy Spirit leading the way, each day, into this uncharted territory for Christ's glory!

Today's devotional was originally written during the weekend of Pentecost—ten days after I finished the original 40 days. Technically, it's Day 41 (I folded the 1st day into this book's introduction). I thought I was done writing, but the LORD impressed upon me to share this bonus devotional. He wants you to know that His Kingdom is coming! He also wants you to know that it is a very REAL place!

Remember... you are ambassadors of God's Kingdom—representing Jesus Christ in this world. With everything that is currently happening in our world and with what awaits on the horizon, we need to KNOW that we belong to Christ and His Kingdom! Our eternal destiny depends on it.

Jesus is worthy of all praise, glory and honor!

34 *"Then the King will say to those on His right, 'Come, you who are blessed by My Father, take your inheritance, the kingdom prepared for you since the creation of the world."* - Matthew 25:34 (NIV)

Jesus did everything—while on earth—with the Kingdom in mind. The danger in this life is that we can become so preoccupied with the cares of the world, that we miss the reality of God's very real Kingdom which will come. Aspects of God's Kingdom CAN be experienced—in part—now. But on the Last Day, when Christ returns to earth, we will begin to know God's Kingdom in all of its fullness! In the meantime, while we wait, God has made it possible for us to contemplate His Kingdom through His Word.

God wants us to meditate on His Kingdom so we can become so taken by it that we begin to live in its reality—now! We need courage to face what is coming upon the world. That courage comes from Christ—the KING of the Kingdom. So, let us take a look at what the Bible says about God's Kingdom—*the inheritance prepared for us since the creation of the world.* Here are 5 Key Points. A Scripture will be given for each, followed by Scripture references, so you can continue the journey of discovery!

ONE: The Kingdom of God has a KING.

"Jesus said, 'My kingdom is not of this world. If it were, my servants would fight to prevent my arrest by the Jewish leaders. But now my kingdom is from another place." -John 18:36

(1 Kings 22:19-22; Psalm 82:; 103:19; 145:11-12; Isaiah 6:1-8; 9:6-7; Daniel 7:9-14; John 6:35-40; Ephesians 1:19b-23; Philippians 2:9-11; Revelation 1:4-6; 4:1-11; 19:11-16; 20:11-15)

TWO: The Kingdom of God has a PEOPLE.

20 *"But we are citizens of heaven, where the Lord Jesus Christ lives. And we are eagerly waiting for Him to return as our Savior.* **21** *He will take our weak mortal bodies and change them into glorious bodies like His own, using the same power with which He will bring everything under His control."* - Philippians 3:20-21

(Daniel 7: 9-10; Matthew 5:10; 19:14; Luke 22:29-30; John 3:3-5; Romans 8:14-17; 2 Thessalonians 1:1-10; 1 Peter 1:4; Ephesians 2:19; 1 Peter 2:4, 9-10, Hebrews 1:14; Revelation 1:5-6; 5:10; 7:9-17; 21:3; 22:14)

THREE: The Kingdom of God is a REALM that has a PLACE (heaven and earth).

2 My Father's house has many rooms; if that were not so, would I have told you that I am going there to prepare a place for you? **3** *And if I go and prepare a place for you, I will come back and take you to be with me that you also may be where I am.* **4** *You know the way to the place where I am going."* - John 14:2-4

(Genesis 1:1; Isaiah 2:1-4; 11:6-10; 25:6-8; 65:17-25; 66:1; Zechariah 14:9; Matthew 6:10; 1 Corinthians 15:22-24; Hebrews 11:10; 13:14, Revelation 11:15; 21:1-4,10-14)

FOUR: The Kingdom of God has an ARMY:

52 *"Put your sword back in its place,"* Jesus said to him, *"for all who draw the sword will die by the sword.* **53** *Do you think I cannot call on my Father, and He will at once put at my disposal more than twelve legions of angels?"* **54** *But how then* *would the Scriptures be fulfilled that say it must happen in this way?"* -Matthew 26:52-54

(Genesis 32:1-2; Joshua 5:13-15; 2 Kings 19:35; Psalm 91:11-12; Matthew 13:41; Judges 5:20; 2 Kings 6:15-18; Rev 19:11, 14, 19)

FIVE: The Kingdom of God has a PURPOSE:

"However, as it is written: 'What no eye has seen, what no ear has heard, and what no human mind has conceived' -- the things God has prepared for those who love him." -1 Corinthians 2:9

(Daniel 2:44; 7:27; Micah 4:1-3; Matthew 4:23; 7:21; 13:11, 47-50; 19:28; 25:21; Luke 12:32; 13:28-29; 19:17; John 3:16; 14:6; Acts 3:19-21; Romans 2:6-8; 14:17; Colossians 1:13; Hebrews 12:22-24; Revelation 11:15; 21:3-4; 22:12-21)

God's purpose is to create a people who will forever be in relationship with Him. Let us hold onto the fact that God has an inheritance waiting for us—His Kingdom! When Christ makes all things new, ALL consequences of sinful corruption will be destroyed forever! The fullness of God's Kingdom will be perfectly experienced by those who are perfected by Christ! Keeping God's Kingdom Truth at the forefront of our minds will help us be faithful witnesses to Christ in every situation. Ultimately, God has won! Because we belong to Jesus... we win too! Maranatha!

PRAYER: Heavenly Father, thank you for preparing a kingdom for everyone who places their faith in You. Please make us ready to receive our inheritance. In Jesus' Name, Amen.

ACTION: Study the Scriptures provided in today's devotional to help you understand more about God's Kingdom which encompasses both heaven and earth.

EPILOGUE

I wanted to close this 40 Day Devotional with the prayer of Jesus recorded in John 17. It's the major prayer He prays before going into the Garden of Gethsemane and being betrayed by Judas and turned over for crucifixion. In it, Jesus prays to His Heavenly Father for Himself, His disciples and every believer in every generation who will believe in Him—that includes you. Read what Jesus prays and take heart knowing that He prayed for you.

JOHN 17 (NIV)

1 After Jesus said this, he looked toward heaven and prayed: "Father, the hour has come. Glorify your Son, that your Son may glorify you. 2 For you granted him authority over all people that he might give eternal life to all those you have given him. 3 Now this is eternal life: that they know you, the only true God, and Jesus Christ, whom you have sent. 4 I have brought you glory on earth by finishing the work you gave me to do. 5 And now, Father, glorify me in your presence with the glory I had with you before the world began.

Jesus Prays for His Disciples

6 "I have revealed you to those whom you gave me out of the world. They were yours; you gave them to me and they have obeyed your word. 7 Now they know that everything you have given me comes from you. 8 For I gave them the words you gave me and they accepted them. They knew with certainty that I came from you, and they believed that you sent me. 9 I pray for them. I am not praying for the world, but for those you have given me, for they are yours. *10* All I have is yours, and all you have is mine. And glory has come to me through them. *11* I will remain in the world no longer, but they are still in the world, and I am coming to you. Holy Father, protect them by the power of your name, the name you gave me, so that they may be one as we are one. *12* While I was with them, I protected them and kept them safe by that name you gave me. None has been lost except the one doomed to destruction so that Scripture would be fulfilled.

13 "I am coming to you now, but I say these things while I am still in the world, so that they may have the full measure of my joy within them. *14* I have given them your word and the world has hated them, for they are not of the world any more than I am of the world. *15* My prayer is not that you take them out of the world but that you protect them from the evil one. *16* They are not of the world, even as I am not of it. *17* Sanctify them by the truth; your word is truth. *18* As you sent me into the world, I have sent them into the world. *19* For them I sanctify myself, that they too may be truly sanctified.

Jesus Prays for All Believers

20 "My prayer is not for them alone. I pray also for those who will believe in me through their message, *21* that all of them may be one, Father, just as you are in me and I am in you. May they also be in us so that the world may believe that you have sent me. *22* I have given them the glory that you gave me, that they may be one as we are one— *23* I in them and you in me— so that they may be brought to complete unity. Then the world will know that you sent me and have loved them even as you have loved me.

24 *"Father, I want those you have given me to be with me where I am, and to see my glory, the glory you have given me because you loved me before the creation of the world.*
25 *"Righteous Father, though the world does not know you, I know you, and they know that you have sent me.* **26** *I have made you known to them, and will continue to make you known in order that the love you have for me may be in them and that I myself may be in them."*

WHAT NOW?

You have just spent 40 days contemplating the teachings of Jesus. This is a major accomplishment! It shows that you have a serious desire to know God and be used by Him on a deeper level. The question is: *what do you do now?* We often read books, gain knowledge and then move on to other things in life. But in order for us to benefit from the knowledge, we have to put it into some kind of meaningful action.

How do you continue to build upon this foundation so that you can grow closer to Christ? How do you dive deeper into God's Word? How can you take what you've learned during this time and have a positive impact on others?

Here are several suggestions to help you move forward. I have placed them within two categories: *Spiritually* and *Socially*.

SPIRITUALLY

ONE: Seek Christ about your next steps. He may have a specific and unexpected assignment for you to do.

TWO: Make sure you complete all of the action steps at the end of each devotional. You never know what "aha" moments may arise as you do them.

THREE: Study the Scripture passages mentioned in this devotional. This will help you to "connect the dots" of Scripture to better grasp God's Grand Narrative.

FOUR: <u>Journal about your reading experience</u>—the insights the Lord has shown you, how they have helped your understanding of Scripture, and have impacted your day-to-day interactions with others.

FIVE: <u>Read the devotional again</u>. It will help to reinforce your understanding and you may even see something new!

SOCIALLY

ONE: <u>Tell others about this book!</u> If it has been a blessing to you, let others know! Word of mouth is still, hands down, the best form of advertising. Please use whatever platform that is available to you to help spread the word. *(phone, text, email, Facebook, etc)*

TWO: <u>Consider purchasing copies for family, friends, co-workers (*and even your enemies*)</u>. Knowledge is truly a gift which keeps on giving. And the greatest form of knowledge any of us can have is about God's love demonstrated through Jesus. The benefits last for eternity!

THREE: <u>Start a book club where you can read this devotional with others and discuss it together</u>. The experience of a group gathering together in a relaxed atmosphere (whether in person or virtually) to discuss a book in detail is invaluable!

FOUR: <u>Let me know how this book has impacted you</u>. Writing and publishing a book is often a one-way phenomenon. Authors do not always get a sense of how their books are impacting readers. Feel free to contact me through my website, <u>APW3.com</u>, and share your thoughts, questions and concerns.

FIVE: <u>Leave a review on amazon.com</u>. Many people read reviews in order to determine whether or not they will purchase a book or other product. Your review can help someone else—you may never meet—to make a decision to buy **The Resurrection Life**. And that decision could help change their life forever!

Also, the more reviews a book gets on <u>amazon.com</u> the greater exposure it receives so more people will learn about it.

Thank you for considering these ways to increase your engagement with this devotional. You are holding in your hands one of the most important books I have written to date. The other is my previous book, **Resurrection: The BIG Picture of God's Purpose and Your Destiny** (Revised Edition).

I believe these books can help all of us—as believers in Christ —to grow in our knowledge and understanding of God's Word, enabling us to have an intimate relationship with Jesus who is the Son of Man of Daniel 7. I also believe these books can help us become better witnesses for Christ as His 2nd Coming draws ever closer.

May God bless you, keep you and guide you each day, for His glory, your good and the good of those around you. In Jesus' Name… Amen.

—Rev. Allen Paul Weaver III, M.Div

READ THE COMPANION BOOK IN THE SERIES:

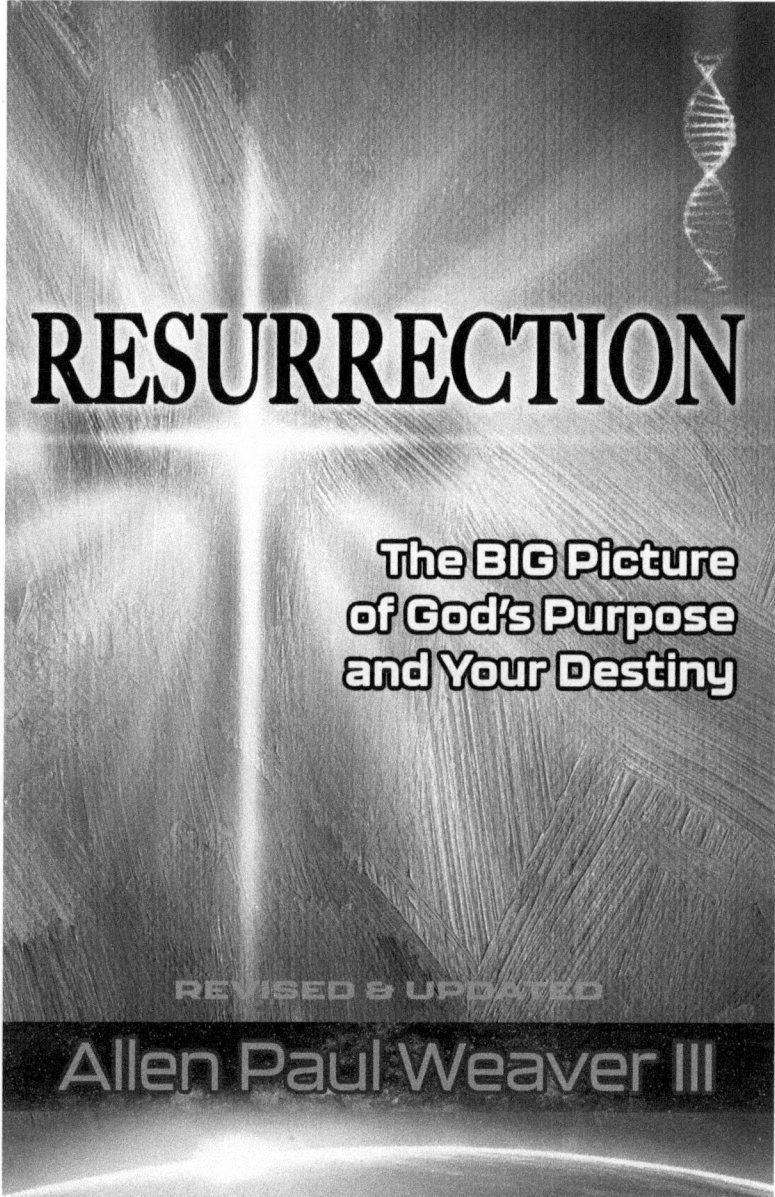

RESURRECTION

The BIG Picture
of God's Purpose
and Your Destiny

REVISED & UPDATED

Allen Paul Weaver III

—RESURRECTION THOUGHTS—

—RESURRECTION THOUGHTS—

—*RESURRECTION THOUGHTS*—

—*RESURRECTION THOUGHTS*—

—RESURRECTION THOUGHTS—

—RESURRECTION THOUGHTS—

ACKNOWLEDGMENTS

I want to say "thank you" to the following people for their assistance with this book:

To my wonderful wife, Ijnanya—Thank you for listening to these devotional entries and providing your feedback. Thank you also for praying over this work and over me. I love you.

To my father, the Rev. Dr. Allen Paul Weaver Jr., —Thank you for providing me with the platform to write and share these devotionals with our church congregation during a very challenging time.

To Dr. Tosha Sampson-Choma—Thank you for taking time out of your busy schedule to edit this manuscript. And thank you for sharing how the words within this book impacted you.

To Rev. Donna Owusu-Ansah—Thank you for assisting me with several last-minute formatting issues. And thank you for your continual creative encouragement over the many years we have known each other.

God has used each of you to help make this work what it is. For that, I am truly grateful! May God continue to bless you in all of your endeavors for His glory.

ABOUT THE AUTHOR

Rev. Allen Paul Weaver III is the author of several books which help readers overcome the obstacles to their God-given dreams and purpose.

His previously published works include **Transition: Breaking Through the Barriers** (autobiographical anthology), **MOVE! Your Destiny is Waiting on You** (personal development), the epic **Speedsuit Powers Trilogy** (young adult fiction) and its followup, **Flight** (young adult fiction), and **Resurrection: The BIG Picture of God's Purpose and Your Destiny** (religion/Christian living). He is currently working on several additional manuscripts for future publication.

Allen earned his bachelors degree in Speech/Mass Communications from Bethune-Cookman University. He earned his master's of divinity degree in theology from Colgate Rochester Crozer Divinity School.

He has been preaching and teaching God's Word in a variety of church and conference settings for over twenty years. Through preaching, teaching, writing and other gifts, Allen seeks to help people discover and walk in their true identity in Christ.

Allen and His wonderful wife, Ijnanya have one amazing son.

Visit www.APW3.com to learn more.